The Book Of Religion And Empire

Ali Tabari

THE BOOK OF RELIGION AND EMPIRE

PUBLISHED FOR THE JOHN RYLANDS LIBRARY AT
THE UNIVERSITY PRESS (H. M. McKechnie, Secretary)
12 Lime Grove, Oxford Road, Manchester
LONGMANS, GREEN AND CO.
London: 39 Paternoster Row
New York: 55 Fifth Avenue
Bombay: 8 Hornby Road
Calcutta: 6 Old Court House Street
Madras: 167 Mount Road
BERNARD QUARITCH LIMITED
11 Gray Street, New Bond Street, London, W.

THE BOOK OF RELIGION AND EMPIRE

A SEMI-OFFICIAL DEFENCE AND EXPOSITION OF ISLĀM WRITTEN BY ORDER AT THE COURT AND WITH THE ASSISTANCE OF THE CALIPH MUTAWAKKIL (A.D. 847-861)

BY

'ALI ṬABARI

TRANSLATED WITH A CRITICAL APPARATUS FROM AN APPARENTLY UNIQUE MS. IN THE JOHN RYLANDS LIBRARY

BY

A. MINGANA, D.D.

OF THE MSS. DEPARTMENT OF THE LIBRARY, AND SPECIAL LECTURER IN ARABIC IN THE UNIVERSITY OF MANCHESTER

MANCHESTER: AT THE UNIVERSITY PRESS
LONGMANS, GREEN & COMPANY
LONDON, NEW YORK, TORONTO, BOMBAY, CALCUTTA, MADRAS
LONDON: BERNARD QUARITCH LIMITED
1922

INTRODUCTION.

I.

The present work may possibly attract the attention of some scholars and students of comparative religion. It is a semi-official defence of Islām written at the command, with the assistance, and in the court of the Caliph Mutawakkil (A.D. 847-861); the adversaries more frequently attacked are the Christians, who, thanks to their numerical strength, to the vigilance of the East-Syrian Patriarchs residing in Baghdad, and to the influence of a successive series of court-physicians, were the strongest opponents of the State religion at the time of the 'Abbasid dynasty; in the second rank come Jews, Hindūs, Buddhists, and Parsees, who, however, are more severely handled. The work is also likely to throw great light on the religious tendencies of Muḥammadanism at the time of its greatest expansion and orthodoxy.

It is not our intention to give here a synopsis of the general plan adopted in the execution of the work, nor to express an opinion on its intrinsic merits and demerits.[1] We leave the reader to draw his own conclusions on the subject; but in order to help him in his task we have

[1] A short essay in this direction was published in *J.R.A.S.*, 1920, pp. 481-488. In some respects it is the weightiest of all the works on Islām that we have read for a long time, and during the last seven years we have perused more than seven hundred Arabic MSS. on different subjects. The author has displayed a literary art which has certain merits of its own, and which, from many sentences such as "if the adversaries shout," appears to have been dictated to him by a series of public discussions held in the court of Mutawakkil.

ventured to add a few short notes to some statements which, to use a sentence of the author's, not two learned men can regard as irrefragable.

The second half of the eighth and the first half of the ninth centuries were, owing to the somewhat tolerant attitude of the Caliphs of Baghdad, marked by the first serious shock of opinion between Christians and Muslims. It was at this time that, in answer to certain objections advanced by Christians, the ingenuity of the Muslim writers gathered from scattered materials and purely oral sources the weapons which in the same field of controversy would place them on even terms with their seemingly more favoured opponents. We do not believe that the imposing number of Muḥammad's miracles and prophecies (with which we should compare Ḳur'ān, xxix 49; xiii. 27-30; xvii. 92-97) would have been so skilfully elaborated at so late a date as the eighth century, if their compilers had not been forced so to act by ready adversaries who had made the subject of thaumaturgy a special point in their polemics against them. We have here and there isolated cases of public discussions before this period. The earliest and the most important record seems to be the colloquy which took place in Syria between the Arab generals and the Monophysite Patriarch of Antioch, John I., in the eighteenth year of the Hijrah Sunday, 9th May, A.D. 639). The Syriac text of this document has been published by F. Nau,[1] and we have given a summary of it in the *Journal of the Manchester Egyptian and Oriental Society* (1916, p. 35 seq.). On the other hand, we know nothing about the discussion between the Umayyad 'Abdul-Malik b. Marwān (A.D. 692-705) and Ibrāhim, son of Rāhib (monk) Ṭabarāni.[2]

[1] *Journal Asiatique*, 1915, 248.

[2] Mentioned by Steinschneider, *Polem. u. Apolog. Liter.* 1877, No. 65, p. 82.

The outcome of the discussion in the second half of the eighth century is known, on the Christian side, by the Syriac writings of Timothy, Patriarch of the East Syrian Church (A.D. 780-823). In one of his letters[1] he records, by way of question and answer, the gist of the public discussion that he had before the Caliph Mahdi, about A.D. 783. At the end of the same century Abu Nūḥ of Anbār, the secretary of the Muslim Governor of Mosul, wrote a refutation of the Ḳur'ān, which Ebedjesu of Nisibis[2] has registered in his *Catalogue*, compiled in A.D. 1298. Assemani mentions a work entitled *Discussion between the monk Abu Ḳārah and the Commander of the Faithful*,[3] and Steinschneider,[4] who has included it in his book as No. 64, believes that this Commander of the Faithful was the Caliph Ma'mūn (A.D. 813-833). This treatise does not seem, however, to be of importance, and it is even possible that it consists of a record by an author of a later date of an event which had taken place several decades earlier; and the same may be said of the above discussion between b. Marwān and Ṭabarāni.

During the reign of Ma'mūn, in whose time the edict against the dogma of the eternity of the Ḳur'ān was issued, the better known *Apology of Christianity* by Kindi saw the light. The exhaustive study of W. Muir[5] renders it unnecessary for us to enter into detail concerning this work, but it would be useful here to remark

[1] I read it in a MS., cf. *al-Machriq* for May and June, 1921.

[2] Assemani, B. O. iii., i., p. 212.

[3] Ibid. iii., i., p. 609.

[4] *Polem. u. Apol. Lit.* p. [illegible].

[5] *Apology of al-Kindy in Defence of Christianity*, London. I read the Arabic text in the edition of the Nile Mission Press, 1912. A recent reviewer in the *Jewish Quarterly Review* has unsuccessfully tried to throw doubts on the authenticity of this book which from internal and external evidence is certainly one of the most genuine compositions that we possess in the literature of the 9th century. Cf. Casanova, *Mahomet et la fin du monde*, ii, *Notes Complémentaires*.

that the present Defence seems to be an attempt to refute lucubrations similar to those of Timothy or Kindi at an interval of some twenty-five to thirty years. The epithet "Garmecite," however, that the author applies to his adversary, points to a man living or born in the region of Mosul or that of the two Zābs, the word used by the author in this connection being *Jurmuḳāni* (cf. p. 81).

Facing the Muslim side, it is worth noticing that the author of the present Defence speaks of some polemical dissertations which in our days seem to be lost (p. 3). It would be interesting also to have more details about the pamphlet entitled *Answer to Christians* by 'Amr b. Baḥr al-Jāhiḍh, the celebrated Mu'tazili writer who died A.D. 869; it is recorded by Ḥajji Khalīfah in his Bibliographical Dictionary,[1] and by Steinschneider;[2] and we have no reliable information concerning the controversial dissertation of Abu 'Īsa Muhammad al-Warraḳ, which occasioned an answer by the monophysite Yaḥya b. 'Adī of Takrīt,[3] who died in A.D. 974. Without dilating on the numerous but not very instructive publications of later generations we may, therefore, venture to assert that the present work, apart from its intrinsic value, is in order of date one of the most ancient.

The historical environment which gave birth to the present Defence is not too complex. The period of religious toleration referred to above was briskly changed by Mutawakkil into an era of recrudescence of Islāmic tendencies. This Caliph, whom Barhebraeus calls "a hater of Christians,"[4] ordered that all churches built since the commencement of Islām should be demolished,

[1] iii. 353.

[2] Ibid. No. 61, p. 73.

[3] Ibid. pp. 128 and 146. See the recent work of A. Périer, *Yaḥia b. Adi, Petits traités apologétiques* (1920).

[4] *Chron. Syr.* p. 155 (edit. Bedjan).

and forbade the employment of Christians in Government offices and the display of crosses on Palm Sunday; he also gave orders that wooden figures of demons should be fixed on their doors, that they should wear yellow cowls, and a zonarion round the waist, that they should ride saddles with wooden stirrups with two globes behind the saddle, that the men's clothes should have inserted a couple of patches of colour different from that of the clothes themselves, each patch to be four inches wide, and the two patches were also to be of different colour. Any Christian woman who went out of doors was to wear a yellow tunic without band.[1] Under these circumstances, it is highly creditable to the author not to have employed a stringent style in his dealings with the "members of the protected cults" (*dhimmis:* said mostly of Jews and Christians). On the other hand, his propensity to flattery is explicable by the pride of Mutawakkil, who was pleased to be described as "the shadow of God spread between Him and His creation,"[2] or "the rope extended between God and His servants."[3]

The promulgation of the edict of the above persecution is ascribed by Ṭabari to 235/849. From the general tenour of the present Defence it is clear, however, that either the persecution had not yet begun when the work was written, or that the work was edited some years after the edict of the persecution was issued, i.e. at a time when, owing to the unpopularity of its enactments, or to the changed attitude of the Caliph himself, it had reached the stage of a slow and natural death. The first hypothesis seems to be irreconcilable with the author's statement on p. 138, and the second would require, as

[1] Ṭabari, 3, 3, 1387 seq., analysed in J. Zaydān's *Ummayyads and Abbasids* (translated by D. S. Margoliouth), p. 169.

[2] Mas'udi, vii. 278-279 (B. de Meynard). [3] Ṭabari 3, 3, 1387.

events moved in the palaces of the Caliphs,[1] a year not far remote from A.D. 855, or six years after the promulgation of the edict of the persecution. This date has the advantage of harmonising with the author's statement on p. 138.

II.

Since this Defence represents the first published work of 'Ali Ṭabari, it will be useful to gather all the available information concerning his life and his works. Unfortunately, historical references to him found in writers of later date are scanty and confused. The very surname of his father, the Syriac vocable *Rabban*, has been read *Zain*, *Zaïl*, *Rain*, etc., by many historians, and this mistake, which can easily be accounted for by the use of early and undotted Arabic letters on the part of Muslim writers, who hardly knew any other Semitic language besides Arabic, has been repeated by some well-known Arabists, in spite of the clear explanation given to it by the author himself in his medical work entitled *Kunnāsh*. This last Syriac word, or its Arabic equivalent *Jāmi'*, was adopted by many Christian and Muslim physicians as constituting the best title to be given to their "complete" repertory of Græco-Oriental physiology and therapeutics or general pathology. Such is the title of two works by John b. Serapion, one by George b. Bokhtishō', one by the priest Aaron, one by Isaac b. Ḥunain, one by Sāhir, one by Rāzi, one by Theodore, etc.[2]

The mention made of Ṭabari by the Islamic authorities may be summarised as follows:

[1] The best work on the life in the palaces of the Caliphs is Miskawaihi's *Tajārib* (or "Experiences of Nations"), translated by D. S. Margoliouth in 1921 (Oxford, vols. i.-iv.).

[2] See *Fihrist*, pp. 296-303.

1. *The General Historians.* The better known compatriot of our Ṭabari, i.e. the famous historian Muḥammad Ṭabari, mentions the author four times, in his *Annales*, under the name: 'Ali b. Rabban, the Christian writer (see 3, 2, 1276-1277; ibid. 1283; ibid. 1293, edit. De Goeje), all in connection with Māziār of Ṭabaristan; and Mas'ūdi in his *Murūj* (viii. 326, edit. B. de Meynard) gives a quotation from him describing a bird called *Kīkam.*

2. *Fihrist* (Flügel, p. 296). "Ali b. Zail,[1] [with a *Lām*] Abul-Ḥasan 'Ali b. Sahl at-Ṭabari. He wrote to Māziār b. Ḳāran. When he became Muslim at the hands of Mu'taṣim, the latter drew him near to himself, and his merits became known in the Court. Then Mutawakkil bestowed honour upon him and made him of the number of his table-guests. He was a literary man and his books are: "*Paradise of Medicine; Gift to the Kings; The Kunnāsh; Utility of Food, Drink, and Medicinal Herbs.*" The author of the *Fihrist*, who was writing about 120 years after the death of Ṭabari, seems to have distinguished him from 'Ali b. Rain, "the Christian" whom he mentions on p. 316 as author of a book on *Literature and Proverbs according to Persians, Greeks, and Arabs.* In reality this 'Ali appears to be identical with the author of this Defence. Further, is not the *Kunnāsh* the same work as that entitled *Paradise of Medicine?* We shall presently see that this book is preserved in some public libraries as having both titles. The British Museum MS.[2] expressly states, "This is the index of the chapters of the *Kunnāsh* of 'Ali b. Rabban, which is entitled *Paradise of Medicine.*"

3. *Ibn al-Ḳifṭi* (edit. Lippert, 1913, p. 231). "'Ali b.

[1] Possibly an error for *Rabl.* Cf. the quotation from b. abi Uṣaibi'ah and b. al-Ḳifṭi given below.

[2] Cod. CCCCXLV. p. 218, in Rieu's catalogue.

Zain[1] at-Ṭabari, abul-Ḥasan, the physician. He excelled in the medical science, and was at the service of the governors of Ṭabaristan. He studied philosophy and devoted himself to natural science. After an insurrection which took place in Ṭabaristan he went to Ray, where he became tutor to Muḥammad b. Zakariā' ar-Rāzi, who learned much from him. Thence he repaired to Sāmarra where he settled and wrote his *Kunnāsh* entitled *Paradise of Medicine*. . . . He is mentioned by Muḥammad b. Isḥāḳ an-Nadīm in his book, in which he says: 'Abul-Ḥasan 'Ali b. Zain, who is b. Sahl aṭ-Ṭabari. Zain is the name of Sahl, because he was a Rabbi to the Jews." This last information is erroneous, because the author of the *Fihrist* clearly states that the father of Ṭabari was a Christian (cf. here pp. 19, 50); further, the reading of "Zain" instead of "Rabban" in this quotation is evidently an error of the copyist, because it is the word "Rabban" and not "Zain" which means *Rabbi.*

4. *Ibn Abi Uṣaibi'ah* (edit. of the press of Wahab, 1882, p. 309). "Ibn Rabban aṭ-Ṭabari, who is abul-Ḥasan, 'Ali b. Sahl, b. Rabban at-Ṭabari. Ibn Nadīm of Baghdad says (that his name was) Rabl, with a *Lām*, and relates about him as follows: He was the writer of Māziār b. Ḳāran; when he became Muslim at the hands of Mu'taṣim, the latter drew him near to himself, and his merits became known in the Court. Then the Caliph Mutawakkil made him of the number of his table-guests. He was a literary man and he instructed Rāzi in the medical profession. He was born and brought up in Tabaristan. Among his sayings is the following: 'An ignorant physician is liable to death.' Ibn Rabban aṭ-Tabari has among other books: *Paradise of Medicine* . . . ; *Gentleness*

[1] This word is rightly corrected into Rabban in the edition of Cairo, A.H. 1326. See pp. 128 and 155.

of Life; Gift to the Kings; The Kunnāsh; Utility of Food and Drink and Medicinal Herbs; Preservation of Health; Enchantment; Scarification; Preparation of Food."

5. *Yākūt* reports in his geographical dictionary (edit. Wüstenfeld, ii. 608): "Something like the above narration has been recorded by 'Ali b. Zain aṭ-Ṭabari, the writer of Māziār. He had acquired medicine, and has works on many subjects." We consulted Yākūt's *Dictionary of Learned Men*, recently edited by D. S. Margoliouth, but were unable to find in it any reference to our author; nor is there any mention of him in Sam'āni's *Ansāb*, an introduction to which was written in 1912 by the same scholar.

6. *Ibn Khallikān* (life, 717, 8, p. 75 of Wüstenfeld's edit.) writes about Rāzi the celebrated physician: "He studied medicine under the physician abul-Ḥasan 'Ali b. Zain aṭ-Ṭabari, who has well-known works, such as the *Paradise of Medicine*. He was first a Christian, then he became a Muslim."

7. Far more important is the following historical notice transmitted by the author himself in his work *Paradise of Medicine*[1] above mentioned: "My father was one of the writers of the town of Merw, and one of the most esteemed and learned men in it. He had a remarkable zeal for the acquisition of piety and the acquaintanceship of those who excelled in it. He was a constant reader of books of medicine and philosophy, and he preferred medicine to the profession of his fathers. His aim in it was not vainglory nor money, but esteem and consideration. He was for that surnamed *Rabban*, which means 'our master' and 'our teacher.'"

[1] Cod. CCCCXLV. of the *British Museum*, p. 217 (Rieu). The work is also found in Cod. 6257 of *Berlin*, v. p. 513 (Ahlwardt), and in Cod. 1910 of *Gotha* iii. p. 456 (Pertsch). Cf. also Cod. DLXVII. of Oxford, p. 135 (Uri).

8. In the MS. containing the present Defence the first leaf, which had begun to fade, has been transcribed afresh by a sixteenth century hand with the following historical note: "This (MS.) has been transcribed from the autograph of the author. 'Ali b. Zain, the writer of this book —may God have mercy on him—says, 'My father was writer to Māziār, the master of Tabaristan.' When Mu'taṣim took Māziār at the hand of 'Abdallah b. Tāhir, ('Ali) asked for safety, and then he became one of the table-guests of the Caliph Mutawakkil 'ala Allah, and beatitude was ascribed to him. He became an eminent scholar, a traditionist, and a man of many works. The book has been transcribed from the autograph of its author, which fact will also be mentioned at the end of the work. It is an excellent book, the merit of which is known only by the man who studies it with care."

In addition to all these references it should be noted that the medical works of Ṭabari are frequently quoted or referred to in books of a later date, under the name "Ṭabari." See Badr ad-Dīn Ḳalānisi's *Ḳarābādīn* (MS. 435 in the John Rylands Library; passim) and Nafīs Kirmāni's Commentary on Najīb ad-Dīn Samarḳandi's *Asbāb wa 'Alāmāt*, where he is sometimes given his full name: 'Ali b. Zain Ṭabari (see fol. 402[a], MS. 221 of the John Rylands Library).

Finally we should record the fact that at the bottom of the first page the titles of the following three chapters of a work by the author are transcribed apparently from an autograph: on the three denominations, the Melchites, the Jacobites, and the Nestorians (p. 110); on the sentences differently worded by the Apostles (p. 126); on the ambiguous letters wherewith they have argued in favour of their laws (p. 131). The work alluded to seems to have been the *Book of Replies to Christians* mentioned on pp. 101 and 107.

These are the original notices about the author, who at the beginning of his Defence calls himself "freedman" of the Caliph Mutawakkil. This might more appropriately be referred to Mu'taṣim (A.D. 833-841), in whose time Māziār b. Ḳāran b. Wandāhormiz of Ṭabaristan was finally defeated by 'Abdallah b. Ṭāhir,[1] and who, according to Barhebraeus, freed at his death-bed eight thousand slaves bought with his money.[2]

That the writer was an eminent physician and moralist is established by the above quotations. He was also the nephew of the Syrian doctor, abu Zakkār Yahya b. Nu'mān, whom he mentions by name, and to whom he attributes a polemical work lost in our days.[3] If abu Zakkār is the same man as Zakariyā' mentioned by Bar Bahlūl in his Syriac lexicon and identified by some critics with abu Yaḥya al-Marwāzi—an identification which to us seems very doubtful—the year of his death should be ascribed to the second quarter of the first half of the ninth century, because the author of this Defence speaks of him in terms which suggest that he had lived shortly before the final edition of his book. Confusion between physicians and moralists of the ninth century is frequent in the works of a later date, and the time has not yet come to speak of them in an irrefragable manner. If we were allowed to add a remark to the identification of Zakarīyā' with abu Yaḥya al-Marwāzi,[4] we should say that an identification with abu Zakariyā' Yaḥya b. Māsuwaih,[5] the physician of the Caliphs Ma'mūn, Mu'tasim, Wāthiḳ, and Mutawakkil, would be more in harmony with the general course of events. On the one hand, the name given to him by the author does not conflict with

[1] Ṭabari, 3, 2, 1268 seq. [2] *Chron. Syr.* p. 153 (Bedjan).

[3] See p. 147. [4] Cf. *Fihrist*, p. 263, and Usaibi'ah i. pp. 234-235.

[5] Cf. *Fihrist*, pp. 295-296, and Steinschneider in Z D M G, 1893, xlvii. pp. 351-354.

this surmise, and on the other hand, the year of his death commonly believed to have been A.D. 854-855 would be in consonance with the text of our Defence, written certainly between 847 and 861, and probably in 855.

III.

THE manuscript which contains the text of this Defence is, so far as we are aware, unique. It is numbered 631 in the Crawford collection of the John Rylands Library, measures 210 × 127 mm. and consists of 73 leaves of paper, with 19 lines to the page. The first leaf, which, as stated above, had begun to fade, has been written afresh by a sixteenth-century hand. If the scribe's statement is correct—and we have no reason to question it—the MS. is a transcript from the author's autograph. This appears in the note translated above, which refers us to the colophon at the end of the MS. Unfortunately, this colophon cannot be deciphered in its totality. The sentences which can be read with safety may be translated as follows:

"The book was finished—and glory and praise be to God—on the morning of Friday 4 Muḥarram of the year six hundred and sixteen—may God make good its beginning! Has copied it for himself the servant soliciting the mercy and the forgiveness of the Almighty God: 'Abdul-Ḥamīd b. Ḥusain b. Bashīḳ, who thanks the Almighty God for His favours and blesses His Prophet, our Master Muḥammad, with his family and companions, and gives them peace for ever."

The date A.H. 616 (A.D. 1219) is also found on the first page, written by the sixteenth-century hand, while at the bottom of the last page the following words are read in a thirteenth-century hand: "I said This is the last work copied by Jamāl ud-Dīn, who died shortly after he had finished it." Can this Jāmal ud-Dīn be identified with the above 'Abdul-Ḥamīd?

On folios 1a, 19b, and 59b, marginal notes dated 1148/1735 1149/1736 bear the name of an owner, a certain Mūsa al-Maulawi. It is evidently this man who has added a few philological and historical notes on the narrow margins of the book, and vocalised some difficult words. These stray notes are the only data that we possess as to the provenance of the MS.,[1] which was apparently written in Baghdad forty years before its sack by the hordes of Hūlakū. From the footnotes of pp. 97, 106, 131, etc., and from some passages of the text, it would appear that the MS. is a transcript from a first or rough draft made by the author, but it is possible to admit that some of these passages were marginal notes which have been misplaced by the copyist.

The translation given in the present volume preserves the Arabic colouring of the original, but contains a few explanatory words not found in the text, and safeguards the interests of a general reader not necessarily an Arabist. We have inserted some foot-notes to elucidate difficult points, and have compared the historical and traditional sayings reported by the author with the following authorities:—

Buk. The *Ṣaḥīḥ* of Bukhāri; edition of Cairo, A.H. 1313, in nine volumes.

Hish. Ibn Hishām's Life of the Prophet; edition of Cairo, A.H. 1332, by Ṭahṭāwi, in three volumes.

[1] The words "In Egypt" are also clearly read at the top of the title-page after a truncated line.

I.S. The *Ṭabaḳāt* of Ibn Sa'd, edited at Leyden under the direction of E. Sachau, in seven volumes.

Musl. The *Ṣaḥīḥ* of Muslim; edition of Cairo, A.H. 1327, in two volumes.

Musn. *Musnad* of Aḥmad b. Ḥanbal; edition of Cairo, A.H. 1313, in six volumes.

Ṭab. The *Annals of Ṭabari;* edited at Leyden under the direction of De Goeje, in fifteen volumes.

Taj. *Tāj al-'Arūs.* Arabic dictionary, edition of Cairo, in ten volumes.

Had we extended our comparisons to all the traditional books, we should have swollen the foot-notes without appreciable advantage.

Other historians and theologians are quoted without abbreviations and with full reference to the edition which we have used.

It must not be inferred that our comparative apparatus implies that the same tradition is registered *verbatim* by the writers referred to in the foot-note. It is a well-known fact that an identical tradition is sometimes so confusedly worded by the authors of the ninth century that the readers can scarcely recognise its extent and purpose, and more especially the occasions and circumstances which gave birth to it. As to the meagre historical value of all this tardy *Ḥadīth*, the reader should consult the recent and well-known publications of Professors Margoliouth, Goldziher, Wensinck, Snouck Hurgronje and Lammens, in the light of which many lucubrations by ancient critics have become antiquated.

With regard to the Biblical quotations found in the book, since the author is mostly dependent only on the Syriac Version, we have collated his translation with the Peshiṭta. This collation is complete so far as the Pentateuch is concerned, but for the rest of the sacred Books a note has been added only in case of a mistranslation or misquotation.[1]

About the author's sources nothing can be stated with any degree of certitude. On the one hand, the historical details in the section dealing with the Prophet and the Orthodox Caliphs, are often preceded by the formulæ "It has come to our knowledge," "It has been related," which may equally point to oral traditions and to written sources. On the other hand, there is no reason for denying the probability that Ṭabari was in the privileged position of having ready access to the archives and the library of the Court in which, it is to be presumed, the few Islāmic biographical works (most of which are now lost) preceding the present Defence, were to be found. On p. 19 the author is speaking of works written from the time of the appearance of Islām down to his own day, and now and then he endeavours to furnish important details of circumstantial evidences; so on p. 34 he states, in connection with a miracle of the Prophet, that the descendants of the man to whom the wolf spoke, were in his own time known by the epithet "the children of the man to whom the wolf spoke."

Concerning a Biblical Version quoted by the author on pp. 78, 95, 98, and attributed by him to a certain Marcus the *tarjamān*, we could find no definite traces. From the *Fihrist* (pp. 23-24) we know that the Old and New Testaments were translated into Arabic long before the tenth Christian century, but we have no reason to identify the problematic Marcus Ya'Ḳūbi called Bādawi, therein mentioned as author of an Arabic book, with Marcus the *tarjamān* spoken of in the present Defence. On p. 306

[1] The reader will doubtless notice the differences in the numbers of the chapters of the Bible used by the author. The numbers of the chapters of his Bible are those formerly in use in the East Syrian (Nestorian) Church.

the *Fihrist* mentions an earlier but still more problematic Marcus.

On the authority of *Cod. Vat. Arab.* 13, of the end of the eighth century, we may state that an Arabic Version of the Gospels was in existence about A.D. 750 (cf. Scholz's *Krit. Reis.* 118 seq., and Guidi's *Ev.* p. 8). Further, the historian Michael the Syrian (edit. Chabot ii. p. 431) attributes an Arabic translation of the Gospels to the Christian Arabs assembled at the above public discussion which took place in Syria in A.D. 639. This, if we mistake not, is the oldest date to which any Christian historian has ascribed the existence of an Arabic Version of the Gospels, but great importance should not be attached to a mere historical tradition without subsequent data of a concrete and positive order.[1]

We believe that the problem of "Marcus, the translator," may be satisfactorily solved in the following manner: in the still unpublished repertory of the East Syrian exegesis, entitled *Gannath Bussamé*,[2] a tradition is registered to the effect that the Hebrew text of the Old Testament was translated into the Syriac Peshiṭta of our days by the disciple Mark, probably Mark the evangelist himself. There is no necessity, therefore, to resort to the hypothesis that the author was dependent in his scriptural quotations upon a pre-existent Arabic Version of the Bible. The Syriac statement of the *Gannath* may be translated as follows:—

"Some people report that Mark himself translated the Old Testament from Hebrew into Syriac, and that

[1] No account has been taken above of the tradition recorded by some writers that Khadījah's relative, Waraḳah, had translated the Gospels into Arabic in the time of the Prophet. We have likewise omitted as valueless some other traditions transmitted in the late *ḥadīth*, the authors of which probably possessed less information than we do on the subject.

[2] Page 260 of Syr. MS. 41 of the John Rylands Library.

he presented his translation to James, the brother of our Lord, and to the Apostles, who appended their approbation to it and gave it to the inhabitants of Syria."

The above tradition had evidently gained an unchallenged credit in the Christian and Muslim circles of the middle of the ninth century.

It is a pleasing duty to express here my sincerest thanks to my colleague, Dr. H. Guppy, the chief librarian of the John Rylands Library, for many good suggestions and for his unfailing kindness in providing the necessary research material to which all the merits of the present work are to be attributed; and to my friend, Prof. D. S. Margoliouth of Oxford for help in the decipherment of some Arabic words which had almost completely faded away.

JOHN RYLANDS LIBRARY,
27th June, 1922.

CONTENTS.

PAGE

I.—PROLOGUE 1

II.

On the Different Forms of Stories and Common Agreements . . 6

III.

Directions for the Verification of Stories 10

IV—CHAPTER I.

The Prophet Called to the Unity of God, and to the same object as that included in the Faith of Abraham and all the Prophets. 20

V.—CHAPTER II.

On the Merit of his Prescriptions and his Laws 23

VI.—CHAPTER III.

The Miracles of the Prophet which have been Denied and Rejected by the *People of the Book* 30

VII.—CHAPTER IV.

The Prophet Foretold Events Unknown to him, which were Realised in his Days 37

VIII.—CHAPTER V.

The Prophecies of the Prophet which were Realised after his Death . 40

IX.—CHAPTER VI.

The Prophet was an Unlettered Man, and the Book which God brought down to him and which He made him Recite is a Sign of Prophetic Office 50

X.—CHAPTER VII.

The Victory of the Prophet is a Mark of Prophetic Office . . 57

XI.—CHAPTER VIII.

Those who Called to his Religion and Witnessed the Truth of his Cause were most Honest and Righteous Men 61

PAGE

XII.

Asceticism of Abu Bakr 61

XIII.

Asceticism of 'Umar Ibnul-Khaṭṭāb 65

XIV.

Asceticism of 'Ali ibn Abu Ṭālib 69

XV.

Asceticism of 'Umar ibn 'Abdul-'Azīz, and of 'Abdallah ibn 'Umar Ibnul-Khaṭṭāb, and of some other Pious Muslims . . . 70

XVI.—CHAPTER IX.

If the Prophet had not Appeared, the Prophecies of the Prophets about Ishmael and about the Prophet who is the Last of the Prophets, would have necessarily become without object . . 77

XVII.—CHAPTER X.

The Prophecies of the Prophets about the Prophet 85

XVIII.

The Prophecies of David about the Prophet 88

XIX.

The Prophecies of Isaiah about the Prophet 93

XX.

The Prophecy of the Prophet Hosea about the Prophet . . . 117

XXI.

The Prophecy of the Prophet Micah about the Prophet. . . 118

XXII.

The Prophecy of the Prophet Habakkuk about the Prophet . . 119

XXIII.

The Prophecy of the Prophet Zephaniah about the Prophet . . 121

XXIV.

The Prophecy of the Prophet Zechariah about the Prophet, which corroborates the Prophecy of Zephaniah 123

XXV.

The Prophecy of the Prophet Jeremiah about the Prophet . . 124

XXVI.

The Prophecy of the Prophet Ezekiel about the Prophet. . . 128

Corollary 129

PAGE

XXVII.

The Prophecy of the Prophet Daniel about the Prophet . . 133

XXVIII.

The Prophecy of the Christ about the Prophet 140

XXIX.

The Answer to those who have said that the "Refugees" and the "Helpers" Embraced the Faith without any Sign . . . 147

XXX.

The Answer to those who have Blamed Islām in one of its Practices or in one of its Prescriptions 153

XXXI.

The Answer to those who reprobate the fact that the Prophet Contradicted Moses and Christ in Changing the Rules of the Torah and the Gospel 158

XXXII.

The Answer to those who have pretended that no one but the Christ mentioned the Resurrection 161

XXXIII.

Conclusion 162

Index 171

I.

PROLOGUE.

IN THE NAME OF GOD THE COMPASSIONATE AND THE MERCIFUL WHOSE ASSISTANCE WE SOLICIT.

SAYS 'Ali son of Rabban Ṭabari, the freedman of the Commander of the Faithful: Praise be to God for the religion of Islām which whoso embraces shall be successful, whoso maintains shall be rightly guided, whoso upholds shall be saved, and whoso impugns shall perish. It is by it that the Creator has been made known; it is for it that nations are craving and souls have longed; it is by it that hope is fulfilled sooner or later, because it is the living light and the crossing to the eternal abode of perfect happiness in which there is no grief nor illusion. God, the Most High, has made us of the number of the people of the *Sunnah*, and has caused us to avoid falsehood and the injuries it brings to its adherents; God is indeed to be praised and blessed, and there is no end to His Kingdom, and nobody can change His words. He is the Benefactor and the Wise who has revealed the truth and enlightened it, and has created His servants, sent His Apostle, His Beloved, and His Friend, to those who were in doubt about Him, calling them to the eternal victory and the shining light.

When the hour came and was near, God, the Most High, sent our prophet, Muḥammad—may God bless and save him—to all creatures, as preacher, warner, and illuminating lamp.[1] He proclaimed the order of his Lord, and overawed his enemies into respect and fear by persuasion and dissuasion, and by imparting to them the

[1] Ḳur. xxxiii. 45.

knowledge of a thorough reformation. He exhorted to heaven and its beatitude, and prevented from being unmindful of hell and its fire. He conveyed on the part of God the revelation which the angel Gabriel communicated to him, and to which falsehood shall not come from before it nor from behind it.[1] He did not set aside any truth that the prophets had brought forth before him, but confirmed and corroborated it, and ordered belief in them and praises in favour of the first and the last of them.

God said in His perspicuous book: "Say, We believe in God, and what has been revealed to us, and what has been revealed to Abraham, and Ishmael, and Isaac, and Jacob, and the Tribes, and what was brought to Moses, and Jesus, and what was brought unto the Prophets from their Lord; we will not distinguish between any one of them, and unto Him are we resigned."[2]

And He said: "The Apostle believed in what has been sent down to him from his Lord, and the believers all believed on God and His angels, and His Books, and His Apostles. We make no difference between any of His Apostles"—and the rest of the verse.[3] And about those who associate gods with God, or give him a companion, He said:

"Say, He is God alone, God the Eternal; He begets not, and is not begotten, nor is there like unto Him anyone."[4] And He said:

"Say, O ye people of the Book, come to a word laid down plainly between us and you, that we will not serve other than God, nor associate aught with Him, nor take each other for lords rather than God. But if they turn back then say, Bear witness that we are resigned."[5] And He said:

"Is he who has laid down his foundation upon the fear of God and His goodwill better, or he who has laid

[1] Ḳur. xli. 42, etc.
[2] Ḳur. ii. 130.
[3] Ḳur. ii. 285.
[4] Ḳur. cxii. 1-4.
[5] Ḳur. iii. 57.

his foundation upon a crumbling wall of sand, which crumbles away with him into the fire of hell? But God guides not a people who do wrong."[1]

It is to these points that his proclamations were directed, it is on them that he founded the edifice of his call, and it is with them that he started the legislation of his religion and the stipulations of his truth which the polytheists among the Arabs, and the holders of the inspired Book have denied. They have hidden his name and changed his portrait found in the Books of their prophets—peace be with them.[2] I shall demonstrate this, disclose its secret, and withdraw the veil from it, in order that the reader may see it clearly and increase his conviction and his joy in the religion of Islām. In that I shall tread a path more direct and advantageous than that opened by some other writers of books on this subject. Some of them have shortened, curtailed, and contracted their argument, and have not explained it satisfactorily; some of them have argued in poetry against the *People of the Book*, and in ignorance of their Books; and some of them have crammed the two faces of their books with addresses to Muslims rather than polytheists, then have put forth their proofs in a most elaborate and difficult discourse. The adversary would be right if he wished to say that these writers resembled a collector of firewood by night, who indiscriminately picks up small and big pieces, or a person carried away in a torrent, who suddenly shouts out unpleasant or refined phrases; and that that with which they argued was not to demonstrate but to conceal, not to enlighten but to blind, not to lessen difficulty but to increase it. He who writes a book on this high, illuminating and enlightening subject which involves a general utility to adherents to all religions, has to make it comprehensible and easy; has to

[1] Ḳur. ix. 110.

[2] Cf. Ḳur. vii. 156, and I. S. i. ii. 89, and i. i. 123 and passim in *Buk. Musl. Hish.*

discuss and compete with his adversary, and not to bully and offend him; he is to be intelligible, and not obscure; courteous, and not abusive; he is to use indulgence, to embellish [the tenor of his speech][1] by making it lucid, and to bring forth proofs and replies which, when addressed [to the adversary],[1] should cause him to abandon his religious claim and his faith. If he does that to him, he will ride on him, hit him with his arrow, and lead him with his bridle.

I have aimed at this by the help of the Most High God, and have made the meanings of my sentences easy, in order that the reader may understand them, and not be in doubt. I did not leave the members of the protected cults any argument, any difficult question, any contentious point, that I have not mentioned and then refuted and solved, by the succour and assistance of God, and by the blessing of His Caliph, the Imām Ja'far al-Mutawakkil 'ala-Allāh, Commander of the Faithful—may God prolong his life—who guided me and made me profit by words heard from him. He is in earnest and eager that such books should be spread and perpetuated in order to strengthen the motives of credibility of the Faith, to make its proofs triumph, and to convince of his merit therein those who ignore it, and do not recognise how God has singled out Islām and its followers in his time and renewed for them His benefits; nor how, through the gentleness of his administration, He has made Himself felt by them, in multiplying, increasing, and honouring them.

I have found that people who have contradicted Islām, have done so for four reasons: *firstly*, because of doubts about the history of the Prophet—may God bless and save him—; *secondly*, because of disdain and egregious insolence; *thirdly*, because of tradition and custom; *fourthly*, because of folly and stupidity. By my life, had

[1] The words between brackets have completely disappeared from the text and have only been guessed.

they discerned and grasped the truth of that history, they would not have rejected it. And since they have sought what is with God, by contradicting the command of God, we must needs decide to prove this history to them, expel doubt from them, and explain to them the origins and the subdivisions of stories, their causes and their courses, and the way to discern their veracity from their falsehood, and the reasons through which and for which people have accepted their prophets and responded to their missionaries. We shall next compare our story with theirs, the men who transmitted ours to us with those who handed down theirs to them; if the proofs that we have for believing in our Prophet are the same as those they possess for believing in theirs, they will have no excuse before God and before their own conscience for disbelieving in our Prophet, though believing in theirs, because if two opponents bring forth the same evidence to establish certain claim, they have both the same right to it, and what is due to one must necessarily be due to the other.

II.

ON THE DIFFERENT FORMS OF STORIES AND COMMON AGREEMENTS.

EVERY story is of two kinds; it is either true or false. It has, also, three tenses; it is either past, or present, or future. Certain stories may be sometimes true and sometimes false; as if you would say: "Such and such a man came or went;" this may be true, and may also be false. Some stories are true at all times, past and future, gone or to come, because they are of the domain of the clear, universal, and common fact; as if one would say, "The firmament has finished its diurnal rotation, or it will finish it to-morrow;" or if somebody says: "The sun rose yesterday, or will rise next year;" or if he says: "The majority of the quadrupeds give milk in bringing forth;" or, "The majority of the birds lay after they have been covered, and hatch when they have laid." These and similar examples constitute a fact, true in its totality, at all times, and are of the category of the first and commonest agreement.

Some stories are wholly false, at all times, past or future, as if one would say: "This has more light than the sun, and is sweeter than honey; This horse is swifter than lightning, or more nimble than a tick;" or if he says: "All people gathered together so that none was left;" or, "Such and such a man is the best of men, and is more learned than all of them; has a precious object worth everything; his country is the most fertile of all the countries created by God." This and similar kinds of speech are wholly false, but they are used by the majority of mankind in their figurative style, and are not considered as wrong.

After this first and commonest agreement that I have mentioned, there is a second common agreement which involves less universality and generality; such is the story of Adam and Eve, and of their being the parents of mankind. This is true for us in an indubitable manner, because of the credence attributed to it by the majority of mankind, and of the testimony borne by prophets to its truth; but it is considered as lie and falsehood by many people, such as the Indians, the Sabeans, and the like.

After this second common agreement, there is a third common agreement which involves less generality and universality; such is the story of the Greeks, the Indians, and the Chinese; because although most people who narrate it are from the low and common class, yet it is true and indubitable, because of the constant agreement and the numerous testimonies that it possesses.

After this third common agreement, there is a fourth one which involves less generality and universality; such is the story of the appearance of Alexander, of the Tabābi'ah, and of the King Jam, and the like; it is accepted as true, because of the great number of people who believe in it; but people who believe in the story of the above-mentioned countries, are more numerous than those who believe in the story of the Tabābi'ah and Alexander.

A fifth common agreement is transmitted to one another by people who adhere to it from a long period, like the story of Buddhists, *Zindīḳs,*[1] and Magians; it is true and indubitable to them, but it is an unmistakable falsity to us; it began with juggleries and quibbles; then through tradition and heredity, habit and custom, it became to them a religion.

That it is a characteristic note of stories to lay easily hold upon mind and imagination is true and undeniable. There are indeed stories which by their queerness please

[1] Manichaeans, Atheists.

the hearer, whose face in listening to them blushes with blood and whose eyes shed tears and blink fast from immoderate laughter. Some of them expel the tears of the hearer, render his body frigid, and cause the radiance of his face to droop; such is the news of unhappy and disastrous events. Some of them excite the hearer to munificence and make him generous to the one who is asking for help and soliciting favour; such is the case of the glorification of generous people and the description of praises and rewards which in exchange for their liberality they receive in this world and in the world to come. Some of them make the hearer avaricious, and turn him away from generosity; such is the news of a man whose extravagance has reduced to poverty and constrained to penury and misery. Some of them incite him to anger and irritation, and make him stretch his hand to strike and his tongue to disapprove. Some of them kindle his passion, move him, and take possession of his eager desires; such is the record of chaste and attractive maidens and the bestowal of encomium on their good qualities, their fragrance, the smoothness of their touch, and the beauty of their smile; especially when this record is adorned with gems of melodies which excite to emotion and infatuation.

Some of them incite people to rush into dreadful things, and to put their life in danger, and that at an interval of more than a thousand years after the death of the first narrator; such is the case of what we are told of the Buddhists of India and of Magians, and the like. Some of the Indians consume themselves with different kinds of burning; some of them expose their body to birds of prey, that they may eat it; some of them wander about like madmen in a waterless desert in order that they may perish therein; some of them throw themselves from a high mountain, and fall upon a tree of iron set up with edged ramifications as sharp as swords and spears—out of zeal for facts handed down to them by some insolent liars who took them from some astute deceivers.

I mentioned these facts in order that the reader may know that he ought to avoid them and to flee from them towards the harbours of wisdom and the ports of thought and consideration. They are indeed most detrimental to the souls, which they affect more swiftly than deadly arrows and vehement passions. They enter the heart from two doors the deceitfulness and delusiveness of which are great, on account of fanciful and unreal conceptions; these are the two senses of hearing and vision, by means of which the insinuations of historical events are grasped. The sense of vision makes sometimes a single object appear as two and a crooked object as straight, like poles in rivers; it makes sometimes a non-existent object as existent, as in illusion and mirage. As to hearing, sometimes one believes a murmuring of the wind to be the thunder; and a simple imitation of a dog, a lion, and a ring-dove, to be the actual whining, or roaring, or cooing.

III.

DIRECTIONS FOR THE VERIFICATION OF STORIES.

I HAVE first spoken of the division of stories and of the strange way in which they impress soul and body through the accidents and happenings of the past. Now what nations have agreed to in their argumentation and considered as thorough investigation and caution, is that when someone is claiming a right, or telling a certain story, if he brings two or three men endowed with sound judgment and discrimination, truth is established and suspicion and doubt are expelled from the judge and the criminal. As to the history of the prophets, its issues being such as to lead to heaven or to hell, we will not be satisfied with two witnesses, nor with an oath, nor with the avowal of a whole community, if account is not taken of the testimonies of truth and the analogical evidences that I shall set forth below.

We have already seen that communities great in number, exalted in rank, and renowned in men of high intellectual and mental acumen bear witness to all the claims laid by many astute liars, as in the case of the *Zindīḳs* and the Magians. This happens either through tradition and habit, as we have shown, or through stupidity and chicanery, or through constraint and compulsion. This Zoroaster, the pseudo-prophet of the Magians, did. He did not cease to wait repeatedly upon King Bishtāsaf until he reached him, and then he threw the seed of his false suggestions into his breast; next, he did not cease to circumvent him by the mention of God and His cult, and to turn round him on all sides in order to remove his refractoriness, until he changed his belief and bent him to his opinions. Then he showed him the Dualism which was in his mind, made good before his eyes the intercourse with mothers and daughters, and the eating of filthy and stinking muck; after that it was the monarch who constrained the inhabitants of his kingdom to his belief.

Mani did similarly. He appeared at a time in which there were generally two religions: Christianism and Magianism. He deceived the Christians by telling them that he was the messenger of the Christ—peace be with Him—and circumvented the Magians by agreeing with them to the two Principles.

After having seen that there is a common agreement such as this, and another one such as that found in Islām, it becomes evident that the acceptance of every common agreement is wrong, and the rejection of every common agreement is an error, and that the common agreement is not sufficient by itself to prove the veracity of a prophetic office, which, indeed, needs signs and marks of truth, such as those God has accumulated in the case of the Prophet—may God bless and save him. He who intends to verify historical events such as these or to redress them, has, therefore, to investigate the story that comes to his knowledge, and to examine its purpose and its defects; if he finds in it and with it something which would contradict it and make it a falsity, no other demonstration is wanted; such is the fact of Musailamah, the liar. When he claimed the prophetic office, he was asked about the Prophet—may God bless and save him—and he answered that he held him to be a speaker of truth and believed in his prophetic office, but the Prophet—may God bless and save him—having been asked about him, denounced him. In the positive answer of Musailamah there was something to negative it; thus he gave the lie to himself, and showed signs of contradiction and stupidity. It is for this reason that learned men have said that when a forger and false dogmatiser claims the prophetic office, God does not give him any respite till from his own tongue there flows the contradiction with which one might argue against those who believed in him; as God has done in the case of Zoroaster, Mani and the like, who contradicted, gainsaid themselves, and became inconsistent.

Zoroaster said that Hormiz—name of their god—was eternal, compassionate, omniscient and omnipotent; then he ascribed to him the description used by ignorant and stupid people, in saying that Satan was born of his mind, and that God was unable to destroy him. Mani, too, did similarly, in saying first that God was eternal, omnipotent, incomparable, and in saying, next, that darkness was eternal, and God would be overcome, and His followers defeated and made captive. He who believes in him who gives the lie to himself is in great error.

So also are the Christians; having said at the beginning of their profession of faith: "We believe in God, creator of every thing visible and invisible," and then adding that the Christ is creator and not created, contradiction appears in their utterances. And if we turn to the Books of their faith, we find that they are not in alignment with their belief, because all of them affirm that God is creator and everything else is created. I have demonstrated this point in the part that follows this, where I have explained what concerns all Christian denominations, and where I have set forth one hundred and thirty arguments against them from the Books of the prophets, apart from rational demonstrations, illustrative examples, and illuminating analogies. In this I have for aim their instruction, their guidance, and the fulfilment of the duty of love and compassion that God has imposed upon some creatures towards one another. As to what concerns the Jews and others, I have treated it in the fourth part in a short but significant manner.

The one interesting point which is treated here and which contains refutations of a restricted dimension and easy, is that of the news reaching an intelligent man of sound judgment, who examines it carefully, and turns it upside down thoroughly; if he finds in it and with it something which would impair its genuineness and contradict it, or if he finds it at variance with the religious Books of the people, he will have no need of anything else for its refutation, and the manifestation of its falsity and groundlessness. When truth is quickly found, the mind is relieved. This Mu'āwiah did with a man from Baṣrah who had asked him for two thousand palm-tree trunks for the erection of his house. Mu'āwiah questioned him: "What are the dimensions of thy house?" The man answered: "Two parasangs by two parasangs." Mu'āwiah asked: "Is thy house in Baṣrah, or is Baṣrah in thy house?" The man answered: "My house is in Baṣrah." Mu'āwiah then said: "All Baṣrah is less than two parasangs." In the story itself there was something testifying to its falsity.

Another man said, while in 'Irāḳ "We were at Ḳūmis,[1] in a garden situated on the western side of the town, at a distance of three hundred parasangs." The man to whom this story was told said: "Therefore, we are now in the middle of that garden, since there is less than this distance between Ḳūmis and 'Irāḳ."

Fākhir said also the same in his book where he prefers Ḳaḥṭān to 'Adnān. After having mentioned that 'Adī, son of Ḥātim, had a son, he added: "Where have you another one like him? His father told him to drive away strangers from his table, but the boy refused, saying: 'Father, command this to other than me.'" And Fākhir said: "The boy is a generous man, son of a generous father, who was himself son of a generous father; and is a magnanimous man, son of a magnanimous father, who was himself son of a magnanimous father." Now I find that the fact itself contradicts his saying. The father had ordered the boy to drive away people from his table; this the boy disliked and rejected; the

[1] In Ṭabaristān.

boy is, therefore, a generous man, son of an avaricious father, and a magnanimous man, son of an ungenerous father.

Let the man who wishes to verify the history of the prophets, and to inquire into it, act likewise; let him examine the testimonies of truth and the analogical evidences, which I have found abundantly existent in ten different manners with regard to the Prophet—may God bless and save him—in such a way that they are not due to anyone but to Christ—peace be with Him. I will explain this point and set it forth clearly, in order that the onlooker may know that he with whom these prerogatives are found, the prophetic office must necessarily be ascribed to him, and a strict accountability to God rests with the man who disbelieves in him:

First, the Prophet—may God bless and save him—called to One, Eternal, Omniscient, and Just God, whom no one can overcome and hurt; in that he was in conformity with all the prophets. *Second*, he was pious, upright, sincere, and his laws and prescriptions are praiseworthy. *Third*, he—peace be with him—wrought clear miracles which only the prophets and the chosen ones of God can work. *Fourth*, he prophesied about events hidden from him, which took place during his lifetime. *Fifth*, he prophesied about many events concerning this world and its kingdoms, which were realised after his death. *Sixth*, he produced a book which by necessity and by undeniable arguments is a sign of prophetic office. *Seventh*, his victory over the nations is also by necessity and by undeniable arguments a manifest sign of prophetic office. *Eighth*, his missionaries who transmitted his history are most honest and righteous men, to whose like nobody can attribute lie and falsehood. *Ninth*, he—peace be with him—is the last of the prophets, and if he had not been sent, the prophecies of the prophets about him and about Ishmael—peace be with both of them—would have been vain. *Tenth*, the prophets—

peace be with them—prophesied about him long before his appearance, and described his mission, his country, his time, and the submission of nations to him, and of kings to his nation.

These are clear prerogatives and sufficient testimonies, which if somebody can show forth as due to him, his arrow will not miss its butt, his truth will triumph, and will have the right to be acknowledged; and he who throws them away and rejects them, his efforts would be fruitless, and this world and that to come would be lost to him. I shall treat this point succinctly, chapter by chapter, and I shall show forth the testimonies of the prophets about it. I shall not restrict myself to one prophet, but I shall appeal to many of them; nor shall I be satisfied with one prophecy, but I shall bring forth more than sixty prophecies. What I most desire is that God should turn my effort to union and admonition, and to outlet from blindness, to anyone who is not insolent and arrogant, nor obstinately set in folly and perverseness.

If we ask especially the Christians why they disbelieve in the Prophet—peace be with him—they would say because of three reasons: *first*, because we do not see that a prophet has prophesied about him prior to his coming; *second*, because we do not find in the Ḳur'ān the mention of a miracle or a prophecy ascribed to the man who produced it; *third*, because the Christ has told us that no prophet will rise after Him. These are their strongest objections, and I will refute them, by the help of God. If I am able to prove that the contrary of what they assert is true, and that for our belief in prophets there is no such necessary condition as that they mention, they will have no more excuse before God and their conscience, and those who adduce such pleas and cling to them are in the path of unbelief and perdition.

The answer to their saying that no prophet has prophesied about the Prophet, and that the prophetic office of the prophets is not true and acceptable except when it is preceded by other prophecies, because he who believes in a prophet who has no previous prophecy about him would be in error and unbelief, is this: let them tell us who prophesied about the prophet Moses himself—may God bless him—or about David, or about Isaiah, or about Jeremiah, who are considered by them as the greatest of the prophets—peace be with them—; and since there is no previous prophecy about them, he who believes in them would, therefore, contradict truth for falsehood, and thus incur the wrath of the Lord of the worlds. The answer to their saying that in the Ḳur'ān there is no mention of a miracle wrought by the Prophet—may God bless and save him—and that he who has no record in his book of a sign or a miracle has no reason to be acknowledged, is this: let them show us the miracle wrought by David and recorded in his Psalter; if they do not find it for us, why and for what reason have they called him a prophet, while no prophet has previously prophesied about him, and there is no record of a miracle in his Book?

From what I have explained it has become evident that, in the process of the verification of the history of prophets, there is no need of a previous prophecy about them, nor of a mention in their books of their miracles or the outward signs of their claims. There are indeed prophets who, as stated above, have in their Books the record of a miracle and a manifest prophecy, but about whom no previous prophet has prophesied; and no one has for that denied their claim; such is the case of Moses, Daniel, Isaiah, and the like—peace be with them. There are also prophets on whom God has bestowed all these prerogatives; such is the case of the Christ—peace be with Him—who has wrought wonderful miracles, foretold hidden and unknown things, and has previous prophecies about Him prior to His appearance. There are prophets who have miracles recorded in their Books, but who did not prophesy; such is the case of Elisha, who gave life to two dead men, but has no direct prophecy. Some prophets, such as Ezekiel and Hosea and others, did not work any miracle, and they prophesied; but their prophecy having been realised long after their death, people who saw them and acknowledged them had no reason for their belief in them, in the absence of a miracle shown by them to their contemporaries. There are some prophets who have in their Books neither miracle nor prophecy, nor convincing stories, and are counted among the prophets; such is the case of Malachi, Haggai, and Nahum, whose Books of prophecies does not exceed three or four pages, for each one of them; such is, also, the case of Miriam the prophetess, Moses's sister, and of Hannah the prophetess, who have neither Book, nor prophecy, nor miracle, nor sign, and they have counted them among the prophets. O my cousins, why and for what reason have you called these prophets?

This being the condition of the Christians, why do they disbelieve in the prophetic office of the Prophet—peace be with him—who actually possesses the above mentioned prerogatives, some of which are perpetuated in the Ḳur'ān, and some in the Tradition, which is of equal value to the Ḳur'ān with the sole difference that those which are contained in the Ḳur'ān afford stronger and clearer argument, and more cogent prophecy. How can they reject them with the explanation that I shall give of the prophecies of the pious prophets about him, and with the allusions of the majority of them to his prophetic office, and to his time—may the peace and the blessings of God be with all of them. If you say that you have rejected and avoided the Prophet—may God bless and save him—because there is no prophet after the Christ, I will make it clear from your own Books that the man who whispered this into your ears and made it flow from your tongues was not an adviser but a deceiver to you, not reliable but suspect.

To this effect, it is written in the eleventh chapter of the Book of the Acts, which contains the Epistles of the

Apostles, that "In those days, prophets came from Jerusalem, and one of them, called Agabus, stood up and prophesied to them that in those countries there will be famine and great dearth."[1] It is said in this same chapter, that "In the church of Antioch, there were prophets and teachers, as Barnabas, and Simon, and Lucius of the town of Cyrene and Manael and Saul."[2] All these five prophets, according to what is recorded, were in Antioch. Some of the women prophetesses are also mentioned. It is said in the nineteenth chapter of this book that "Philip the interpreter had four daughters prophetesses."[3] Luke said, too, in the book of the Acts, that the group going to Antioch "Went to the house[4] of Judas and Silas, because they also were prophets.[5]

The Christians are therefore short of evidence for their claim, and their saying is incoherent, and their arguments have been refuted and overthrown; it has become evident that after the Christ there were people whom they have called Apostles and Prophets; such is the case of Paul himself.

I shall now, by the help and assistance of God, explain the ten prerogatives which I have set forth. I shall present in each chapter what is perpetuated in the Ḳur'ān, as a reproach against those who pretend that there is no mention of a miracle in it. I wish the reader of this book to realise its merit and the excellence of its value, and to know that those born in the religion of Islām and firmly attached to it, who have prefusely dealt with this subject, did not reach what I have attained; he who has a doubt in his breast, let him compare my book, the prophecies, the convincing and peremptory proofs which it contains, the riddles and the

[1] Acts xi. 28. [2] Acts xiii. 1. [3] Acts xxi. 9.

[4] The translator has misunderstood the Syriac particle *dibaith*, which means *partisans*, *companions*, and has rendered it literally by the word *house*.

[5] Acts xv. 32.

intricacies of the adversaries which I have carefully examined, with all that other writers have written, since the appearance of Islām down to our own time. This is due to the help and assistance of God, and to the blessings of the Commander of the Faithful—may God strengthen him—and to the obligations which God imposes through him on his friends and freedmen. It is he—may God prolong his life—who called me to this work, guided me in it, and convinced me that on account of it I shall be entitled to a great reward from God and a good memory from man. Before I became Muslim I was neglectful, led astray, unaware of the right direction, and groping my way far from what later was disclosed to me. Thanks and blessings be to God who has lifted up the veil from my sight, opened the locks for me, and saved me from the darkness of error!

IV.

CHAPTER I.

THE PROPHET—PEACE BE WITH HIM—CALLED TO THE UNITY OF GOD, AND TO THE SAME OBJECT AS THAT INCLUDED IN THE FAITH OF ABRAHAM AND ALL THE PROPHETS—PEACE BE WITH THEM.

The most trustworthy witness to this is the Ḳur'ān, which shows that the Prophet—peace be with him—called only to the God of Abraham, Ishmael, Isaac and Jacob, to the unity of God, and to what pious prophets had proclaimed and sound minds had demonstrated. Among other things, God the Most High, said in the Ḳur'ān:

"Say, He is God alone; God the Eternal; He begets not and is not begotten, nor is there like unto Him any-one."[1] And He said:

"God bears witness that there is no God but He, and the angels and those possessed of knowledge, standing up for justice. There is no God but He, the mighty, the wise."[2] And He said:

"Say, O God, Lord of the Kingdom, Thou givest the kingdom to whomsoever Thou pleasest, and strippest the kingdom from whomsoever Thou pleasest; Thou honourest whom Thou pleasest, and abasest whom Thou pleasest; in Thy hand is good. Verily, Thou art mighty over all."[3] And He said:

"How can ye disbelieve in God, when ye were dead and He made you alive, and then He will take your life and then make you alive again, and then to Him will ye

[1] Ḳur. cxii. 14.
[2] Ḳur. iii. 16.
[3] Ḳur. iii. 25.

return."[1] About the excellence of God, His mercy and His justice, He said:

"Whoso does right it is for his soul, and whoso does evil, it is against it, for thy Lord is not unjust towards His servants."[2] And He said:

"And he who gains a good action, we will increase good for him thereby; verily, God is forgiving and grateful."[3] And He said:

"And he who does the weight of an atom of good shall see it, and he who does the weight of an atom of evil shall see it."[4] And He said:

"What befalls thee of good it is from God, and what befalls thee of bad it is from thyself."[5] And He said:

"God will not require of the soul save its capacity; it shall have what it has earned, and it shall owe what has been earned from it."[6] In exalting the grace of God and His compassion for His servants, He said:

"Verily, God would not wrong by the weight of an atom; and if it is a good work, He will double it, and bring from Himself a mighty reward."[7] And He said:

"We did not wrong them, but they wronged themselves."[8] And He said:

"And when they swerved, God made their hearts to swerve; for God guides not the people who work abomination."[9] And He said:

"That is because they believed and then disbelieved, wherefore is a stamp set on their hearts so that they do not understand."[10] And He said:

"He who brings a good work shall have ten like it; but he who brings a bad work shall be recompensed only with the like thereof, and they shall not be wronged."[11] And He said:

[1] Ḳur. ii. 26.
[2] Ḳur. xli. 46.
[3] Ḳur. xlii. 22.
[4] Ḳur. xcix. 7-8.
[5] Ḳur. iv. 81.
[6] Ḳur. ii. 286.
[7] Ḳur. iv. 44.
[8] Ḳur. xi. 103.
[9] Ḳur. lxi. 5.
[10] Ḳur. lxiii. 3.
[11] Ḳur. vi. 161.

"How will it be when we have gathered them together for a day whereof there is no doubt, when each soul shall be paid what it has earned."[1]

This is the faith of Adam, of Noah, of Abraham, and of all the prophets and righteous men—may God's blessings be with them; and the adversaries do not doubt and suspect it.

[1] Ḳur. iii. 24.

V.

CHAPTER II.

ON THE MERIT OF HIS PRESCRIPTIONS AND HIS LAWS.

As to the dictations and prescriptions of his religion, they are: love of God the Most High; love of parents; strengthening of the ties of relationship; generosity with one's possessions; devotion to gratuitous benefactions; asceticism; fasting; prayer; general alms; legal alms; forgiveness of the culprit; fulfilment of engagements; avoidance of deceit and falsehood; getting rid of wrongs by the kindliest way; prohibition of intoxication, immorality, adultery, and usury; ordinances for spreading safety and justice; striking off the head of recalcitrant unbelievers; and other points without which there is no firm religion and world. Among other things is the following saying of the Most High God:

"For those who expend in alms, in prosperity and adversity, for those who repress their rage, and those who pardon men; God loves the kind."[1] And this other saying:

"Those who expend their wealth by night and day, secretly and openly, they shall have their reward with their Lord. No fear shall come on them, nor shall they grieve."[2] And He said:

"Take to pardon and order what is kind, and shun the ignorant; and if an incitement from the devil incites you, then seek refuge in God; verily, He both hears and knows."[3] And He said:

"And twist not thy cheek proudly, nor walk in the land haughtily; verily, God loves not every arrogant

[1] Ḳur. iii. 128. [2] Ḳur. ii. 275. [3] Ḳur. vii. 198-199.

boaster; but be moderate in thy walk, and lower thy voice; verily, the most disagreeable of voices is the voice of asses."[1] And He said:

"He will not catch you up for a casual word in your oaths, but He will catch you up for what your hearts have earned."[2] And He said:

"Say, I have no power over myself for harm or for profit, save what God will."[3] And He said:

"God desires for you what is easy, and desires not for you what is difficult."[4] And He said:

"Verily, men resigned and women resigned, and believing men and believing women, and devout men and devout women, and truthful men and truthful women, and patient men and patient women, and humble men and humble women, and almsgiving men and almsgiving women, and fasting men and fasting women, and men who guard their private parts and women who guard their private parts, and men who remember God much and women who remembér Him,—God has prepared for them forgiveness and a mighty reward."[5] And He said:

"Verily, God bids you do justice and good, and give to kindred their due, and He forbids you to sin, and do wrong, and oppress; He admonishes you, haply ye may be mindful."[6] And He said:

"And obey not any mean swearer, a back-biter, a walker about with slander; a forbidder of good; a transgressor, a sinner; rude, and base-born, too."[7]

God did not leave a question which would edify and reform His servants, nor a counsel which would tend to please Him, without having spoken of it.

What shows the merit of the divine call of the Prophet—peace be with him—is that he extended his proclamation to all mankind, without sending a special and

[1] Kur. xxxi. 17-18.
[2] Ḳur. ii. 225.
[3] Ḳur. x. 50.
[4] Ḳur. ii. 181.
[5] Ḳur. xxxiii. 35.
[6] Ḳur. xvi. 92.
[7] Ḳur. lxviii. 10-13.

particular invitation to some people to the exclusion of others, as the rest of the prophets had done, except the Christ—peace be with Him. Indeed he generalised his call and promised pardon and heaven to all. Other prophets struck blindly with the sword those who were round them, and squandered their fortune, without calling, forgiving, edifying and warning, as the Prophet—may God bless and save him—was commanded to do.

As to the asceticism of the Prophet—may God bless and save him—his austerity, and his disregard of the allurements and deceitfulness of this world, I will relate some facts from which it will be inferred that from a man of his devotion and temperance no one conceives deceit and falsehood. It has been related of him—peace be with him—that it was only after much pain and anxiety that he ate sufficiently bread or meat.[1]—When he—may God bless and save him—gave his daughter Fāṭimah for marriage to 'Ali—may God be pleased with both of them—the only dowry that he gave her was a bed woven with twisted palm-leaves, a pillow of skin stuffed with palm-tree fibres, an earthen pot, a water-skin, and a basket containing some raisins and dates.[2]—'Ayeshah—may God be pleased with her—said: "We used to stay forty days without firelight." Having been asked on what they lived, she answered: "On water and dates."[3]

Fāṭimah would grind herself the grains for flour; her hands became sorely hurt, and traces of the handle of the mill were seen in them;[4] she complained of that to the Prophet—may God bless and save him—and asked him for a servant to serve her; and he answered her: "My little daughter, I have not in my house a place to contain all the Muslim women of whom you are one; therefore remember and thank God frequently."—He—peace be with

[1] Cf. I. S. i., ii., 114-119. *Musl.* ii. 531.
[2] *Musn.* i. 84, 93, 104, 108.
[3] I. S. i. ii. 114-119. *Buk.* iii. 167; viii. 107. *Musl.* ii. 531.
[4] *Musn.* i 96, 106, 123, 136.

him—would fasten tightly a stone on his stomach out of hunger, eat sitting on the ground, put, when sleeping, his hand under his head as a pillow, and wear his mantle and say: "I am a servant, I eat and sleep like a servant."[1]—He, too—may God bless and save him—would produce from his weeping, while in prayer, a noise resembling that of the boiling of a cooking-pot.[2]

Among the traditions referring to the magnanimity of his conduct—peace be with him—and to the gravity of his character, is that the angel Gabriel—peace be with him—came to him and said: "O Muḥammad, I brought thee the magnanimity of conduct of this world and of the world to come: thou shouldst join with the man who broke with thee, give to the man who deprived thee, and forgive the man who wronged thee."—And he said: "Visit the sick, give food to the hungry, and take away the chains from the captives."[3] He—may God bless and save him—forbade tittle-tattle, frequent questions, and extravagance.[4]—In commanding moderation and content in one's condition, he—peace be with him—said: "The Holy Spirit has whispered in my mind[5] that a person will not die until he has completely provided for his livelihood."—And he said: "He who visits the sick is upon the palm-trees of Paradise."[6]—And he—peace be with him—said: "I am not for games and pleasures, and games and pleasures are not for me."[7]

And he said in praise of asceticism: "He who accumulates wealth will come in the day of judgment having over his eyes a scald-headed snake with two black specks."[8]—And he—peace be with him—said: "Fear the Fire by giving alms, although it be but one half of a

[1] Cf. *Buk.* v. 120, viii. 105. *Musl.* ii. 193. Jāḥiẓ, *Avares*, 240, 241, 242 (edit. Van Vloten). I. S. i. ii. 114, 159.

[2] Lane's *Lexicon*, i. 52.

[3] *Buk.* iv. 71; vii. 130.

[4] Cf. *Buk.* passim in *Riḳāḳ*.

[5] See Lane, iii. 1188.

[6] *Musl.* ii. 383. For this tradition see *Tāj.* vi. 81.

[7] See Lane, iii. 862.

[8] Cf. *Tāj.* v. 393.

date."[1]—And he said: "I stood in the door of heaven, and I saw that those who entered through it were generally the poor, while the rich were cast in prison."[2]

He, too—peace be with him—would say: "God has mercy on the man who owes his safety to his silence, or speaks when speech is necessary for success."—It is related also of him—peace be with him—that he never compelled anyone to give anything; that he never asked anything from anyone, except for the sake of God; and that no one ever asked him anything without his giving it to him for the sake of God.[3]

What the Most High God has prescribed and laid down to his people in the matter of prayers, ablutions, and preliminary preparations dealing with washing after excretion, cleansing the teeth, rinsing the mouth, and other purifications; attendance to public prayer with humble devotion, silence, keeping of ranks, quiet, reiteration of genuflexion and prostration, and utterance of words at each genuflexion and prostration, in order that their knowledge might extend to everybody, little or grown up, male slave or female slave,—all this is as something due to the dignity and the majesty of the Creator, when His servant is present before Him and asking from Him.

It is related also of him—peace be with him—that one day, on the occasion of a temporary interruption of his revelations, he told some people who were present with him: "How can revelations not be interrupted when you do not trim your nails, nor clip your moustache, nor cleanse your finger-joints."[4] He, too—peace be with him—would say: "No human speech fits prayer, which is only for glorification, praise, and reading of the Ḳur'ān." This was against the deed of those who came

[1] *Musl.* i. 375. *Hish.* ii. 93. *Buk.* iv. 207; viii. 122, 126. *Musn.* i. 388, 446.

[2] Cf. *Buk.* iv. 122; viii. 105, 124. See also *Musn.* i. 224, 355; ii. 175.

[3] Cf. I.S. i., ii. 92. *Musl.* ii. 290.

[4] *Musn.* i. 243.

to it when stinking with foul smell or polluted, and those who interrupted their prayers with talks, games, spitting, and eructation.

It is related also of the Prophet—may God bless and save him—that, speaking on behalf of the Most High God, he said: "I have prepared for my servants what eye has not seen, ear has not heard, and the heart of a man has not conceived; except that with which I have made them acquainted."[1]

Among the things which make his religion easy and free from restraint is what God has ordered, through him, about the meal at daybreak, the shortening of prayer for the sick and the travellers, and his saying that the three days following the Day of Sacrifice should be for eating, drinking, and making use of marriage.

One of the marks of the merit of his religion, and of the reasonableness of the prescriptions of the Ḳur'ān, is that we find that the Torah which is in the hands of the *People of the Book* says: "Everyone who kills should be killed." Now Moses himself—peace be with him—and David, and other prophets as well as kings of the Children of Israel, have killed many people, but they have not deserved to be killed. The Ḳur'ān limits and defines that in saying: "And whoso kills a believer purposely, his reward is hell, to dwell therein for aye."[2] It has been related of him—peace be with him—that he said: "He who slays a person with whom he is on terms of peace, will not perceive the odour of Paradise."[3] This is a restricted, limited, corrected, and polished order.

Moses and Jesus—peace be with them—said: "Every claim is settled by two or three witnesses;" so the Jews and the Christians say. But it happens that the two witnesses are wicked and liars; God, therefore, said

[1] 1 Cor. ii. 9; Is. lxiv. 4. This well-known tradition of Bukhāri is well catalogued in *Tāj* ix. 380.

[2] Ḳur. iv. 95.

[3] *Buk.* iv. 103; ix. 14. See Lane, iii. 1178.

through the Prophet—may God bless and save him—"And bring as witnesses two men of equity from among you."[1] In this He limited and enlightened the point at issue with a short, significant, important, and clear saying.

Moses—peace be with him—ordered the children of Israel to curse openly, by the tongue of the nation, anyone who transgresses or neglects something from the laws and the prescriptions of the Torah; but it happens that the one who had transgressed some of them, or had trespassed and committed shortcomings against them, repents and shows penitence, and is no more worthy of curse. Therefore, the Ḳur'ān says: "Those who when they do a crime, or wrong themselves, remember God and ask forgiveness for their sins—and who forgives sins save God?—and do not persevere in what they did, the while they know; these have their reward: pardon from their Lord, and gardens beneath which rivers flow, dwelling therein for aye; for pleasant is the reward of those who act like this."[2] These are messages and points which demonstrate that the man who laid them down was sound, steadfast, pious, devout, and was not a a plagiarist, an appropriator of others' rights, nor one making light of things and lacking gravity.

[1] Ḳur. lxv. 2.

[2] Ḳur. iii. 129-130.

VI.

CHAPTER III.

THE MIRACLES OF THE PROPHET—MAY GOD BLESS AND SAVE HIM—WHICH HAVE BEEN DENIED AND REJECTED BY THE *PEOPLE OF THE BOOK.*

I WILL only relate the miracles of the Prophet—peace be with him—which afford ground for argument with equitable people. I will begin the subject with what is found in the Kur'ān, in order that the adversary may not say that if the Prophet—may God bless and save him—had wrought a miracle, it would have been mentioned in it, in the same manner as the miracles of Moses and Jesus—peace be with them—are recorded in the Torah and the Gospel.

Among his miracles which took place in his time—peace be with him—and to which the Ḳur'ān bears witness, is that he was transferred in a single night from the Sacred Mosque to the Remote Mosque;[1] and this is the saying of the Most High God:

"Celebrated be the praises of Him who took His servant by night from the Sacred Mosque to the Remote Mosque, the precinct of which we have blessed, to show him of our signs."[2]

The Arabs rejected this, saying: "When and how could he cover in a single night the distance which takes two months to go and return?" Then, Abu Bakr—may God be pleased with him—went to him and asked him about it. And he—peace be with him—said: "Yes; and

[1] The Commentators believe that these terms refer to the Ka'bah of Maccah and the temple of Jerusalem respectively.

[2] Ḳur, xvii. 1. See the Commentators.

I encountered the caravan of such and such a tribe in such and such a valley; one of their camels had bolted away, and I directed them to it. I met, too, with the caravan of such and such a tribe, while they were asleep; I drank water from one of their vessels; their caravan is now coming preceded by a dusky camel carrying two sacks, one black and the other black and white." People rushed towards the caravan route, and behold, the caravan was coming preceded by a dusky camel; and they could not find an objection to his miracle.[1] By my life, it is a clear and sufficient miracle, recorded in the Ḳur'ān and accepted by the unanimity of the Muslims.

Among the Prophet's miracles which God has mentioned in His Book, is that when the polytheists harmed him and sneered at him, He said to him: "Therefore, publish what thou art bidden, and turn aside from the idolaters; verily, we are enough for thee against the scoffers."[2] This, too, is found in the Kur'ān, and there are not two men who hold discordant views about it and about its interpretation; it is that five persons of high standing among the polytheists were sneering at him and harming him. Gabriel—peace be with him—came and said to him: "When they make the circuit of the holy house, ask what thou wilt from God, and I will do it against them as punishment." One of them, Lahab son of Abu Lahab, met him in the circuit, and the Prophet—may God bless and save him—said: "Let God's dog eat thee;" and a lion devoured him. Then, Walīd ibn Mughīrah met him, and the Prophet—may God bless and save him—made a sign to a wound that he had in the sole of his foot, and it became recrudescent and killed him. Then, Aswad ibn 'Abd Yaghuth met him, and the Prophet made a sign to his belly; and he became dropsical and died. Then, Aswad ibn Muṭṭalib met him, and he threw a leaf on his face, saying: "My God, blind him, and cause his son to die;" and all this happened to him. Then 'Āṣ ibn Wā'il

[1] *Hish.* ii. 7.

[2] Ḳur. xv. 94-95.

met him, and he made a sign to the hollow of his foot, and a thorn entered into it and killed him. Then, Ḥārith ibn Ṭalāṭilah met him, and he made a sign to him, and he burst out with pus and perished.[1] It is in this way that the Prophet—may God bless and save him—was delivered from the *Scoffers*, who were men of high standing and chiefs of the tribe.

It has been related on the authority of Āminah, the mother of the Prophet—may God bless and save him—that when he fell from the womb she saw light coming out with him, and that he fell on all fours, his face and sight being directed towards heaven.[2]

Among his resplendent miracles noticed by all who saw him in the *Day of Badr*, is that he threw dust on the face of the polytheists and said: "Confusion seize their faces!"[3]; and they fled and were killed.

Anas ibn Mālik—may God be pleased with him—has reported that he heard the cry of a man saying "O Apostle of God!—the houses have been destroyed by the violence of the rain;" and he—peace be with him—said: "Let it fall round us and not upon us." And Anas said: "I saw with my eyes the clouds moving away from the town."[4]—He, too—may God bless and save him—said once to the polytheists who were present with him: "If any of you can pronounce the name of his father or of his brother, I am a liar;" and none of them was able to pronounce it.—Two handfuls of dates were brought to him in the *Day of the Ditch*, and he ordered that they should be laid before him. His herald cried to the army, and everybody ate and was satisfied.—In the *Day of Badr*, the sword of

[1] See the Commentators Zamakhshari and Baiḍāwi on Ḳur. xv. 94, possibly quoting *Hish.* ii. 13.

[2] Cf. I.S. i. i. 63, 97. *Hish.* i. 155. *Tab.* 1, 2, 968-9.

[3] See the historians of Badr—Lit. "Faces have become ugly." See also *Musn.* i. 368.

[4] I.S. i. ii. 117. *Hish.* i. 255. *Buk.* ii. 34.

'Ukkāshah ibn Miḥṣan was broken, and he said: "O Prophet of God, my sword is broken;" and the Prophet—peace be with him—took the stem of a plant used as firewood and gave it to him, and said to him: "Shake it;" and 'Ukkāshah shook it, and it became a sword, with which he went forth and fought; and later, it remained with him all the time.[1]—And he, too—peace be with him—took a pebble, which he moved with his hand, and it praised God; then he put it in the hand of Abu Bakr, and it praised; then he put it in the hand of 'Umar, and then in the hand of 'Uthmān, and it praised in their hands.

It is reported on the authority of Ibn 'Abbās—may God have mercy upon him—that a man on a foray took the nestlings of a bird. The bird came to the Apostle of God—may God bless and save him—and flapped its wings near his head, then it fell in his hands. The Prophet—peace be with him—said: "Who took the nestlings of this bird? Fetch them and give them back to it." They found them with a Muslim, and gave them back to it.

It has been related that a camel knelt on his hands, then bellowed. The Prophet—may God bless and save him—called its owner and said: "This camel has complained and told me that it was with thee since its youth; and thou workedst with it; but now that it was old thou wishedst to kill it." The man answered: "It has told the truth, O Prophet of God, because I am not feeding it."[2]

It has been related, too, that Banu Ghifār wished to slaughter a calf, which spoke and said: "O Children of Ghifar! a happy event! a crier is crying in Maccah 'There is no God but Allah;'" and they left it and went to Maccah, where they found that the Prophet—may God bless and save him—had appeared; and they believed in him.[3]

[1] I.S. i. i. 125. *Hish.* ii. 225. [2] Cf. I.S. i. i. 124.
[3] Cf. I.S. i. i. 102-103. *Hish.* i. 201.

It has been related that a wolf made a raid on some sheep; the shepherds said one to another: "Are you not amazed at this wolf?" The wolf spoke and said: "You are more to be amazed at than I; a prophet has appeared in Maccah calling to God, and you do not answer him."[1] All these are well-known facts among all Muslims, who do not deny anything from them because they did not take place behind closed doors. What corroborates the miracle of the wolf is that the children of the man to whom the wolf spoke are called down to our own day "The children of the man to whom the wolf spoke;" they transmit the fact among themselves, and they are traced back to it, in order that it may not be forgotten, and that no one may have a reason to discredit it.

And he—peace be with him—invoked curses upon the Arabs, and rain was withheld from them, and the land was affected with drought. It has been told, too, of him—peace be with him—that he apprised Abu Sufyān of a secret affair which had taken place between him and his wife Hind. Abu Sufyān was amazed at that, and said to himself: "She has disclosed my secret; I will surely pound her hand on her foot." But the Prophet—may God bless and save him—said: "Do not commit any injustice against Hind; she has not published any secret." Then Abu Sufyān said: "I had suspected her and was perplexed about her; but since thou hast told me what I was telling to myself, I ascertained that she is innocent of what I suspected her."

Among the noted miracles of the Prophet—peace be with him—is the fact handed down by Anas ibn Mālik, who said: "My mother took dates mixed with butter and curd and sent them to the Prophet—may God bless and save him—praying him to eat from them. The Prophet—may God bless and save him—stood up and said to his friends: 'Let us start.' When my mother noticed the crowd, she said 'O Apostle of God, I have

[1] Cf. I.S. i. i. 114. *Buk.* iv. 182.

only prepared something sufficient for thy food, thine alone.'" And Anas said "The Prophet—may God bless and save him—called for divine blessing, and said to me 'Get in the crowd in companies of ten;' and they ate their fill and went out; and we, too, ate, and were satisfied."[1]

It has been related on the authority of Ya'la ibn Umayyah[2] that the Prophet—may God bless and save him—being once on a journey, wished to make his ablutions, and said to me "Go to those two trees and tell them that the Apostle of God—may God bless and save him—commands them to draw near each other." And the two trees came furrowing the ground until they reached each other; the Apostle of God—may God bless and save him—made then his ablutions between them, and ordered them to go back to their place; and they went.[3]—It has been related, too, that a Jew invited him to dinner, and offered him a poisoned sheep; but he—peace be with him—said: "This sheep tells me that it is poisoned." The Jew avowed that, and said: "I wished to test thee and said to myself 'If he is a prophet, the matter will not be hidden from him, but if he is an impostor, he will eat of it, and I will rid people of him.'"[4]

It has been related on the authority of Jābir ibn 'Abdallah al-Anṣāri, who said: "We set off on a journey with the Prophet—may God bless and save him—and we were very thirsty. We hurried towards him, and there was with him a drinking vessel in which there was water. He put his hand in it, and caused the water to jet out of his fingers, as if there were springs. We

[1] Cf. *Buk.* (passim). *Musl.* ii. 192. Cf. also I. S. i. i. 117, and i. ii 124.

[2] A notable man in the province of Yaman, and according to *Ṭab.* (i 3, 1253), the first Chronologist.

[3] Cf. I.S. i. i. 112; *Musl.* in *Sirah.*

[4] I.S. i. i. 113-114; ii. ii. 6-7; iv. 104. *Buk.* iv. 104; vii. 157 *Musl.* ii. 246. Cf. *Musn.* i. 397.

drank and quenched our thirst, and made our ablutions; and we were four hundred men."[1]

This is enough for this work; had we intended to exhaust the subject, the book would have been too bulky; but in what has been written there is remedy for the man whom God wishes to guide and to save. Some of it is taken from the material found in the Ḳur'ān itself, and some of it is taken from the men from whom the Muslims took the Ḳur'ān, and who are considered as reliable in all that is handed down to the nation from them. They resemble in that the Apostles of the Christ—peace be with Him—who transmitted to the Christians portions of the Gospel, and handed down to them the history of the Christ. Therefore, if those men are reliable and worthy of confidence in transmitting his history, they are not to be suspected in all that they have related of him; but if they are not reliable in that point, they are to be suspected in all that they have transmitted, and are deceivers, first of themselves, and then of all men.

[illegible] *Musl.* ii. 278-279, and 543. *Musn.* i. 251, 324, 402. I.S. i. i. 117-118, 121. Cf. *Ṭab.* 1, 4, 1703.

VII.

CHAPTER IV.

THE PROPHET—PEACE BE WITH HIM—FORETOLD EVENTS UNKNOWN TO HIM, WHICH WERE REALISED IN HIS DAYS.

We will begin this chapter also with what is found in the Ḳur'ān, in order to strengthen our argument and destroy the excuses of the adversaries. The Most High God said to His Apostle—may God bless and save him—"Ye shall verily enter the Sacred Mosque, if God please, in safety with shaven heads and cut hair, ye shall not fear."[1] And they entered it when he was still alive, as God had said.—And He said: "And when those who misbelieve were crafty with thee to detain thee a prisoner, or kill thee, or drive thee forth; they were crafty, but God was crafty too, for God is the best of crafty ones."[2] And it happened as God had said, and they wished to be crafty with him, but God thwarted their craftiness, and foiled their stratagem.

And God said: "O Ye who believe! remember God's favours towards you when hosts came to you, and we sent against them a wind and hosts that ye could not see."[3] With them God struck the infidels in the face; and it happened as He had said.—And He said: "We will cast dread into the hearts of those who misbelieve; strike off their necks then, and strike off from them every finger tip."[4] And it happened as God had told him, and he did to them what he was ordered to do. And He said: "Dost thou not look on those who were

[1] Ḳur. xlviii. 27.
[2] Ḳur. viii. 30.
[3] Ḳur. xxxiii. 9.
[4] Ḳur. viii. 12.

hypocritical, saying to their brethren, who misbelieved amongst the People of the Book, 'If ye be driven forth, we will go forth with you; and we will never obey anyone concerning you; and if ye be fought against we will help you.' But God bears witness that they are surely liars. If they be driven forth, these will not go forth with them; and if they be fought against, these will not help them; or if they do help them, they will turn their backs in flight; then shall they not be helped."[1] It happened as God had said to his Prophet—may God bless and save him—because those men have been driven forth, and these their brethren did not go forth with them; and they have been fought against, and they did not help them.

What can a man say against these miracles, while the Ḳur'an mentions them and the Muslim community bears witness to their veracity, and all its members subscribe to their authenticity, and men and women converse about them? If, while they are contained in the Ḳur'ān, it is allowed to consider them as false and revile them, we will not believe the adversaries who say that the Torah and the Gospel do not contain falsehood to which the eye-witnesses of events had deliberately shut their eyes. If then this cannot be said about the Torah and the Gospel and their contemporaries, it is not allowed with regard to the Ḳur'ān and its holders.—About the breakers of faith from the polytheists of Ḳuraish, the Most High God said: "Fight against them! God will torment them by your hands, and disgrace them, and aid you against them, and heal the breasts of a people who believe;"[2] and it happened as He said.

Among authentic stories is the one transmitted by Sa'd ibn 'Ubādah as-Sā'idi, who said: "We were on a foray with the Prophet—may God bless and save him—and with us there was a man who would kill every polytheist against whom he came to fight. We mentioned

[1] Ḳur. lix. 11. [2] Ḳur. ix. 14.

this to the Prophet—may God bless and save him—and he said, "Is he not from the people of the fire?" And Sa'd added "I did not cease to follow him, in order to see the end of his story. He was wounded, and considering death too slow, he put his sword on his navel, and pressed himself against it until he killed himself."[1]

It is related, too, of him—peace be with him—that he said to Khālid ibn al-Walīd and his friends when he sent them against Ukaidir of Dūmat Al-Jandal: "You will find him on the roof of his house, directing cows," and they found him in that state. It has been related, too, of him—may God bless and save him—that his she-camel went astray, and he began to ask for her. The hypocrites said: "This Muḥammad claims to know the secrets of heaven, and he does not know where his she-camel is." He knew upon what they were communing with themselves, and said: "I know but what my Lord tells me; and he has told me that my she-camel is in such and such a valley, her head entangled in a tree." They sought for her and found her in such a state.[2]

It has been related of him—may God bless and save him—that one day he gathered the people and announced to them the death of Najāshi, King of the Abyssinians, prayed for him, and said four times "God is most great."[3] In that very day there came the news of his death, while the sea was separating him from the land of the Abyssinians, and Maccah was not a highway like the highways of East and West.[4]

[1] *Buk.* iv. 74; viii. 136. [2] *Hish.* iii. 335.

[3] Cf. *Buk.* v. 56.

[4] The Prophet having apparently announced the death of Najāshi while at Madīnah and not at Maccah (*Ṭab.* 1, 4, 1720) the author here wishes only to convey the idea that the shortest way from Abyssinia to the former was through the latter.

VIII.

CHAPTER V.

THE PROPHECIES OF THE PROPHET—PEACE BE WITH HIM—WHICH WERE REALISED AFTER HIS DEATH.

WE will begin this chapter also with the prophecies of the Prophet—may God bless and save him—which are mentioned in the Ḳur'ān, in order that no argument may be left to the people of incredulity and obstinacy upon which to lean, nor a hold at which they may clutch. Among other sayings is the following of the Most High God: "Have we not expanded for thee thy breast? and set down from thee thy load which galled thy back? and exalted for thee thy renown?"[1] That is to say, his name shall be invoked and mentioned after that of God in every sermon, enchantment, discussion, marriage, prayer, and the like.

Among other sayings is the following of the Most High God: "When there comes God's help and victory, and thou shalt see men enter into God's religion by troops; then celebrate the praises of thy Lord, and ask forgiveness of Him, He is relentant."[2] In this Sūrah he foretold the nearness of his death to his nation, and what was to take place after him, on the subject of people entering by troops and in masses into his religion; and this was realised. The adversaries look at it after a long time, and they do not deny it.—And the Most High God said: "A. L. M. The Greeks are overcome in the nighest parts of the land; but after being overcome they shall overcome in a few years."[3] And it happened as he said, in a war between Chosrau and Cæsar, and it became evi-

[1] Ḳur xciv. 1-4. [2] Ḳur. cx. 1-3. [3] Ḳur. xxx. 1-2.

dent to the Arabs that his revelation was true. This was incessantly spoken of by them, by their children and their women, in their houses, and they were expecting it and seeking information concerning it until it was noticed by one and all.

And He said, too: "God promises those of you who believe and do right that He will give them the succession in the earth as He gave the succession to those before them, and He will establish for them their religion which He has chosen for them, and give them after their fear, safety in exchange."[1] This is also a prophecy which has been fulfilled and realised, and no one can find a way to deny it, because God has given to the Muslims the succession of the earth, established for them their religion, and changed their fear into safety. What miracle and what prophecy are truer and clearer than these?

And He said, too: "He it is who sent His Apostle with guidance and the religion of truth, to make it prevail over every other religion, averse although idolaters may be."[2] God and His Apostle—peace be with him—proved right, and his religion has prevailed over every other religion, and the adherents of every religion have submitted to him.—And He said, too, to the Arabs who had lingered behind: "Ye shall be called out against a people endowed with vehement valour, and shall fight them, or they shall become Muslims. And if ye obey, God will give you a good reward; but if ye turn your backs, as ye turned your backs before, He will torment you with grievous woe."[3]

These were men who had fallen away from the Prophet—may God bless and save him—to whom he foretold that they would fight against the Greeks and the Persians, unless these become Muslims. This happened as it is in the Ḳur'ān, and the onlookers bear witness to its veracity. What can the adversaries say about these

[1] Ḳur. xxiv. 54. [2] Ḳur. ix. 33. [3] Ḳur. xlviii. 16.

prophecies, and what answers and arguments can they find against them when they are realised, fulfilled, and spread manifestly East and West? And if a scoffer holds them in contempt, or is not satisfied with them, and is resolved to refute and contradict them, he will not destroy except his own soul, will not irritate except his own Lord, will not change except his own fate, and will not be able to find for us in his own Books except what is like them.

Among indubitable traditions it is related that the Prophet—may God bless and save him—said: "I have five names: I am *Muḥammad;* and *Aḥmad;* and *Effacing,* by means of which God effaces infidelity; and *Gatherer,* who will gather people; and *Final,* that is to say, the last of the Prophets."[1] His saying—peace be with him—was fulfilled, and by him God has closed prophecies, and blotted out infidelity, that is to say, He weakened and lessened it, in effacing it from the middle and the heart of the earth, and in leaving a shadow of it in its ends and borders.—It has been related, too, that he was on a mountain, which shook under him; he said to it: "Be quiet; there are only on thee a Prophet, a Just man, and a Martyr;"[2] there were with him Abu Bakr, for whose sake he named "Just man," and 'Umar and 'Uthmān, who were martyred after him. And he—peace be with him—would say to his friends: "I have the precedence over you to the pool;"[3] and God took him before them.

And he—peace be with him—said to Fāṭimah—may God be pleased with her—in the illness of which he died: "Thou wilt follow me more quickly than any other of my

[1] I.S. i. i. 65. *Buk.* iv. 194. *Musl.* ii. 301. *Ṭab.* 1, 4, 1788.

[2] *Musn.* i. 187, 188, 189.

[3] *Buk.* viii. 132. *Musl.* ii. 283. "The Pool of the Apostle" is that of which the Prophet's people will be given to drink on the day of Resurrection (*Tāj.* v. 23). See also *Musn.* i. 257, 402, 406, 439, 453, 455. Its description is in ii. 162.

relatives."[1] And from his relatives she was the first to die after him.—And he said to 'Ali, son of Abu Ṭālib—may God be pleased with him—in pointing to his head and to his beard: "This will be tinged with that."[2] Afterwards, 'Ali was affected with a dangerous illness, and his relatives said to him "We are anxious about thee from this illness." And he said "I do not fear it, because the Apostle of God—may God bless and save him—said to me: 'This will be tinged with that.'" And this, too, was realised, because 'Ali recovered from that illness and was struck on his head with a sword, and killed.—And he—peace be with him—said to 'Uthmān: "God will clothe thee with a shirt; and the people will force thee to take it off; but do not yield." When 'Uthmān was besieged, and the people bade him take off the caliphate, he said to them: "The Prophet—may God bless and save him—told me so and so, and for that I shall not do what you are saying;" and he was killed.[3] And he—may God bless and save him—said to 'Ammār ibn Yāsir: "A rebellious band will kill thee."[4] And he was killed in a battle between 'Ali and Mu'āwiah. And Mu'āwiah did not deny this tradition, but said: "It was not my troops who killed him; but the man who deceived him and made him go forth to fight, he killed him."

And he too—peace be with him—said to Zubair ibn 'Awwām: "Thou shall fight against 'Ali, and in that thou shalt be unjust towards him." He did so, and 'Ali reproached him.—And he—may God bless and save him—said to his wife 'Āyeshah—may God be pleased with her—"The dogs of Ḥaw'ab will bark against thee." When she went to Baṣrah, she heard barking in her night journey; and she asked about the place, and she was answered: "It is the watering-place called Ḥaw'ab." She remembered his saying—peace be with him—and she said "Verily to God we belong, and verily unto Him we

[1] *Musl.* ii. 341. I.S. ii. ii. 40.
[2] *Musn.* i. 102.
[3] Cf. I.S. iii. i. 46. *Tāj.* iv. 428.
[4] Cf. *Musn.* ii. 164.

return,"[1] and repented that she had travelled there.[2]—And he—peace be with him—used to say about Ḥasan son of 'Ali—peace be with both of them—"This my son is a *Sayyid* and God will reconcile through him two Muslim parties."[3]

And he—peace be with him—said: "The earth has been collected together for me, and I saw its Eastern and Western parts, and the empire of my nation will reach the spot from which it has been collected together for me."[4]—He also seized a pickaxe, in the *Day of the Ditch*, and with it he struck a flint which had defied those who were digging; a spark came out of it, and he—peace be with him—said "In this spark I saw the cities of Chosrau." Then he struck another blow, and another spark came out; and he said "In it I saw the cities of Caesar. Verily God will give them to my nation after me."[5]—It has been told of him—peace be with him—that at the end of a journey he would worship and perform two *rak'ahs*,[6] and repair to Fāṭimah—may God be pleased with her. He went to her after he left the *Ditch*; and she began to weep and to kiss his mouth; and he said to her: "O Fāṭimah, why art thou weeping?" And she said "O Apostle of God, I see thee shabby, weary, and clothed in worn out garments." And he said "O Fāṭimah, God has revealed to thy father that it is He who places dignity or lowliness in every house, be it of clay or of hair; and He has revealed to me that my lowliness will be of short duration.[7]

It has been related that Anas ibn Mālik said: "I was in a walled garden with the Prophet—may God bless and save him—and I heard a knock at the door; and he said to me 'O Anas, rise and open the door to the comer,

[1] A sentence of the Kur'ān (ii. 151) proverbial on the occasion of a misfortune.

[2] *Ṭab.* 1, 6, 3109. [3] *Buk.* ix. 62. [4] *Tāj al 'Arūs (s.v.).*

[5] Cf. *Ṭab.* 1, 3, 1467-9, and *Hish.* ii. 73.

[6] Genuflexions at prayer.

[7] Lit. until it reaches where night has reached.

and declare to him that he will go to heaven, and tell him that he will be set over my community after me.' And I went, and lo! I was face to face with Abu Bakr—may God be pleased with him—and I declared to him what I had heard, and I went in. Then another man knocked at the door, and he said 'Rise and open the door to him, and tell him that he will go to heaven, and that he will be set over my community after Abu Bakr.' I opened the door, and lo! I was with 'Umar—may God be pleased with him—and I did what I was commanded to do. Then I heard another knock at the door, and he—peace be with him—said to me 'Rise and open the door to the new comer, and tell him that he will go to heaven, and that he will govern the community after 'Umar;' and lo! I was with 'Uthmān—may God be pleased with him."[1]

It has been related of him—peace be with him—that he used to say: "The death of this generation shall not take place before you have seen people whose faces are like two-fold shields."[2] He, too—may God bless and save him—would say: "Which is the most sterile of your countries?" And they answered: "Khurāsān." And he said: "It will be a source of blessings for you after me." None of the sons of this 'Abbāsid dynasty and of others ignores that Abu Muslim[3] started without any doubt that victory and Caliphate were due to this 'Abbāsid house. When he approached Ḥīrah, he sent a messenger to ask after the members of the family of Abul-'Abbās who were there. When the messenger saw them, he questioned them "Which of you is the son of 'Ḥārithıyah?"[4] and

[1] *Buk.* v. 9, 14; ix. 60. *Musl.* ii. 321. Cf. *Musn.* ii. 165.

[2] *Buk.* iv. 44, 206. *Musl.* ii. 505. *Musn.* i. 4, 7.

[3] The Khurāsānian ringleader of the revolution which overthrew the Umayyad dynasty in favour of the 'Abbasids.

[4] A feminine gentilic from Ḥārith, the tribe of the mother of Abul-'Abbās *Saffāḥ* of the following note. Her father was called 'Ubaidallah b. 'Abdallah, b. 'Abdal-Maddān, b. Dayyān al-Ḥārithi. (See *Ṭab.* iii. 88, and 2499).

this was Abul-'Abbās,[1] the Commander of the Faithful—may God forgive his sins—because it was told in the Tradition that the first one who would become Caliph would be the son of Ḥārithīyah; this they did not suspect. What is more wonderful is that the Umayyads did not doubt that the Caliphate would go to its owners from the members of this house, and for that they were killing them and tracking them under every stone. Meantime the inhabitants of Khurāsān were sending messengers to them, when they were at Sharāt, to strengthen their hope. They did not question the justice of their cause, and when those of them who have been killed were killed, victory dawned in the time decreed by God in traditions handed down to us.

It has come to our knowledge that Abul-'Abbās received the news of the conquest of Yaman and of Sind[2] in the same day; and he showed a great sorrow. His household said to him: "O Commander of the Faithful! it is a day of joy; what does this sorrow mean?" And he said to them "Have you then forgotten the tradition transmitted from the Prophet—may God bless and save him—that the man who would conquer Yaman and Sind in one day, his death would be near." He had fever on that very day, and died some days later.

It has been related of the Prophet—may God bless and save him—that he wrote two letters begun with the mention of his name, one to Chosrau and the other to Caesar, and called them to Islām.[3] As to Caesar, he put his missive on the pillow, and wrote him an answer couched in civil language. As to Chosrau, he tore up his missive and

[1] Abul-'Abbās surnamed *Saffāḥ*, the first 'Abbāsid Caliph (A.D. 750-754).

[2] Sind was conquered by the Muslims in the time of Ḥajjāj (Yāḳūt, *Geogr. Dict.* iii. 166). Evidently the author refers here to the conquest of Sind and Yaman to the 'Abbasid cause (cf. *Ṭab.* iii. i. 80); about the invasions of Sind see Belādhorī's *Futūḥ*, pp. 431-446 (edit. Goeje).

[3] Cf. *Buk.* i. 22; iv. 46; vi. 9. *Musn.* i. 243, 263, 305. *Musl.* ii. 81. *Ṭab.* 1, 3, 1571, etc.

wrote to Phirūz the Dailamite,[1] when still in Yaman, bidding him repair to the Prophet—may God bless and save him—seize him, and slay him. And the Prophet said: "O my God! tear up his kingdom;" and his kingdom was torn up, as you see. And Phirūz went and informed the Prophet—may God bless and save him—of the order he had received about him. The Prophet—may God bless and save him—said to him: "My Lord has informed me that thy lord has been slain. Do not touch me until the news is verified by thee." The news reached them, and Phirūz became Muslim on account of what he had seen and heard; and he called to Islām the Persians who were in Yaman, and they became Muslims. And when 'Ansi, the liar, appeared in Yaman claiming the prophetic office, the Prophet—may God bless and save him—wrote to Phirūz ordering him to kill him. And Phirūz entered his house when he was asleep, bent back his neck, pounded it, and killed him.—He, too—peace be with him—said, "The Caliphate will not cease to be in the family of Ḳuraish."[2]

And the Prophet—may God bless and save him—said to 'Abbās, his uncle, who had brought to him his young son 'Abdallah—may the grace of God be with both of them—"This boy will be the most learned of my nation in religion, and the best versed in the interpretation of the Revelation." He prayed over him, spat in his mouth, and said: "O my God, make him versed in religion, and teach him Interpretation." And he became as he was told, and he was for that called the *Habr*.[3]

Among the evidences of the favours which God confers on the Prophet—peace be with him—and on all who believe in him, is the fact, transmitted by noted and well-known traditions, of 'Umar ibn al-Khaṭṭāb asking water

[1] A governor established by the Sasānian Kings of Persia (*Ṭab.* I, 4, 1763; 1857-1867. *Hish.* (i. 67-68) ascribes a similar incident to Bādhan, about whom see *Ṭab.* I, 4, 1851-1853.

[2] *Buk.* iv. 188; ix. 68. *Musl.* ii. 107.

[3] *Buk.* v. 29, and in 'Ilm. Cf. *Musl.* ii. 351. "Ḥabr" means *priest, doctor.* See also *Musn.* i. 266, 269, 315, 335, 359.

from Heaven in the name of 'Abbās son of 'Abdul-Muṭṭalib—may God be pleased with both of them—in the *Year of Drought.*[1] He took him by the hand, went forth, and said: "O my God! we come to Thee, asking water from Thee through the intercession of the uncle of Thy Prophet." They did not discontinue until a cloud mounted up, which sent a copious rain.[2]

And he used to say to his companions: "By the One who has sent me with truth, although evening finds you humble, you will shine so as to become stars by means of which people will be guided, and so that it will be said: So-and-so has related that he heard the Apostle of God—may God bless and save him—say such and such a thing;" and you see that this happened as he said.

It has been related, too, that 'Ikrimah, son of Abu Jahl, when still idolater, killed in battle a man from the *Helpers;* and the Prophet—may God bless and save him—smiled. A man from the *Helpers* said to him: "Didst thou smile, O Apostle of God, because one of thy kin killed one of us?" He answered: "No; but I smiled because both of them have the same rank in heaven." And 'Ikrimah became Muslim afterwards, and was slain in the action of Ajnādain in the country of the Greeks.[3]—And he—peace be with him—said to 'Adī, son of Ḥātim: "O 'Adī, become Muslim, and thou wilt be safe. O 'Adī, I think that what impedes thee from this is the poverty which thou findest in those who are round me, and the conspiracy through which men have become one band against us. Hast thou seen Ḥīrah?" 'Adī said "No." And he said: "The time is near when from there a woman will travel on a camel without escort to make the circuit of the holy house; and verily, the

[1] Or: *of Ashes.* In the 17th or 18th year of the Flight there was no rain for a long time, and men and cattle perished in great number. (*Ṭab.* 1, 5, 2570 et seq.)

[2] Cf. I.S. iii. i. 232.

[3] This battle is described by *Ṭab.* 3, 4, 2306-7, etc.

treasures of Chosrau, son of Hormiz, will be open to us, three times."[1] And 'Adī added: "I saw myself all that the Prophet—peace be with him—had foretold."

And Abu Bakr—may God be pleased with him—said, when the Arabs turned from Islām[2] and he sent troops against them: "The Apostle of God—may God bless and save him—has promised the Muslims victory and conquest from God, and God will make his religion prevail over every other religion; and God will not fail in His promise." God has, indeed, confirmed and realised the prediction and the saying of the Prophet—may God bless and save him—and every doubt has been expelled.

[1] *Buk.* iv. 207.

[2] This defection is well described by *Tab.* 1, 4 1871 seqq.

IX.

CHAPTER VI

THE PROPHET—MAY GOD BLESS AND SAVE HIM—WAS AN UNLETTERED MAN, AND THE BOOK WHICH GOD BROUGHT DOWN TO HIM AND WHICH HE MADE HIM RECITE IS A SIGN OF PROPHETIC OFFICE.

AMONG the miracles of the Prophet—may God bless and save him—is the Ḳur'ān. It has, indeed, become a miracle of meanings, which no writer of books on this subject has tried to explain without recognising his incompetence and renouncing his discourse and his claim to such an explanation. When I was a Christian, I did not cease to say in accordance with an uncle of mine who was one of the learned and eloquent men among Christians, that rhetoric was not a sign of prophetic office on account of its being common to all nations. But when I waived tradition and customs, and broke with the promptings of habit and education, and examined the meanings of the Ḳur'ān, then I found that the question was as its holders believed it to be. I have never met with a book written by an Arab, or a Persian, or an Indian, or a Greek, which contained, like the Ḳur'ān, unity, praise, and glorification of the Most High God; belief in His Apostles and Prophets; incitement to good and permanent works; injunction for good things, and prohibition of evil things; exhortation to heaven and restraining from hell. Who has ever written, since the creation of the world, a book with such prerogatives and qualities, with such influence, sweetness and charm upon the heart, and with such attraction, felicity, and success, while its producer, the man to whom it was revealed, was unlettered, not even knowing how to write, and having no eloquence whatever? This is without doubt and hesitation a mark of prophetic office.

Moreover, I found that all books worthy of everlasting fame do not fail to deal either with the world and its inhabitants, or with religion. As to the books of literature, philosophy, and medicine, their aim and purpose are not like ours, and are not counted among books of revelation and religion. As to the books dealing with religion, the first one to name, and the first one which came into existence, is the Torah, which is in the hands of the *People of the Book*. Now we find that it deals commonly with the genealogies of the Children of Israel, their exodus from Egypt, their halts and their departures, and the name of the places in which they halted; and it contains, too, high laws and prescriptions which dazzle the mind, and which the intellectual capacity and power of men are unable to comprehend. What the Ḳur'an contains from these historical events is as a reminiscence of the days of the favours of God, as edification, warning, and admonition. As to the Gospel which is in the hands of the Christians, the greater part of it is the history of the Christ, His birth and His life; and with that it contains good maxims of morality, remarkable advices, sublime wisdom, and excellent parables, in which, however, there are only short and small portions of laws, prescriptions, and history. As to the Book of the Psalms, it contains historical events, praises, and hymns of high beauty and sublime character, but it does not contain any laws and prescriptions.

As to the Books of Isaiah, Jeremiah, and other prophets, the greater part of them deals with curses to the Children of Israel, with the announcement of the ignominy reserved to them, with withholding favours from them, inflicting punishments and chastisements on them, and with other kinds of evils.

The wicked *Zindīḳs* have used abuses and invectives

against these Books, saying: "The Wise and the Merciful could not have revealed such things, nor have ordered the prescriptions dealing with the sprinkling of blood on the altar, and on the garment of the priests and the *imāms;* with the burning of bones; with the obscenities and garbage mentioned therein; with persistency in anger and wrath; with the order to desert the houses when their walls shine with white, because this would be a leprosy affecting these houses;[1] with the command to a group of Israelities to march one against another with unsheathed swords, and to fight with endurance amongst themselves, until they had perished in striking and beating one another.[2] The Jewish people put this into action and did not rebel, and they agreed without flinching to endanger their life and perish. People who do these things with promptitude are obedient and not rebellious, friends and not enemies; and friendly and obedient people do not deserve to be ordered to kill and to destroy one another."

Then Moses—peace be with him—ordered that they should go to two mountains close to each other, and that six tribes from them should ascend one mountain, and six tribes another mountain, and that some men from them[3] should read, one by one, the prescriptions and the laws of the Torah and say: "He who transgresses these prescriptions, or neglects them, or loses something from them, is cursed." The tribes who were on the other mountain answered with *Amen* to those who were cursing in a loud voice.[4] Moses did not leave any of them without curses, and even instigated them to curse their successors after them; and they did it promptly, obediently, and without opposition. In that they were led to discomfiture before they were fixed in their homes, and to a general curse before they could perceive the odour of victory and happiness.

[1] Cf. Levit. xiv. 33 seq.

[2] Exod. xxxii. 27-28.

[3] The Levites.

[4] Cf. Deut. xxvii. 11 seq.

Of the same kind is the saying of the Prophet Ezekiel, that God told him to shave his head and his beard with a sharp and keen sword.[1] Similar is the saying of the Prophet Hosea, that God commanded him to marry an adulteress woman, who brought him forth two children; and ordered him to call one of them *I will not have mercy* and the other *They are not my partisans*, "in order that the Children of Israel might know that I will not have mercy on them, and will not consider them as friends and partisans."[2] And Hosea, too, said on behalf of God about the Jews, that their mother was an adulteress, and that they were born of an illegitimate union.[3] One of the prophets also said to the Jews, on behalf of God, that their mother was pleased with the males of Egypt.[4] And after a sermon to the Children of Israel, Isaiah said that he who told this was the Lord whose light is in Zion and furnace in Jerusalem.[5]

Not a single letter resembling such things is found in the Ḳur'ān, which is interwoven with the Unity of God, hymns, praises, prescriptions, laws, history, promises, threats, persuasion, and dissuasion; with prophecies and announcements concerning good things congruous to the majesty of God, His wisdom, and His might; with the consolidation of hope in His forgiveness, His mercy, and His acceptance of repentance; and with other questions by which souls are encouraged, and hopes fearlessly confirmed. God, indeed, says in it: "Verily God is forgiving and merciful; and who forgives sins except God?"[6] And He says, too, "O my servants who have been extravagant against their own souls, be not in despair of the mercy of God; verily, God forgives sins, all of them; verily, He is forgiving and merciful."[7]

[1] Ezek. v. 1.
[2] Hos. i. 2 seq.
[3] Cf. ibid.
[4] Cf. Ezek. xvi. 26.
[5] Isa. xxxi. 9.
[6] Ḳur. iii. 129.
[7] Ḳur. xxxix. 54.

It is right to state that this book is a sign of prophetic office, because there has not been a book similar to it since the beginning of the world, and since the time wherein people began to write on parchment. Moreover, it possesses other striking prerogatives full of light and mystery; viz. other books, and especially those written by philosophers, have been written by literary and scientific men, after meditation and deep thought, and after they had been brought up in towns, heard facts, and conversed with learned men. But the Prophet—may God bless and save him—was not like them, but he was an unlettered *Abṭaḥi*[1] who had not learned from an Egyptian, or a Greek, or an Indian, or a Persian, and had not frequented the sittings of literary men in search of literature or for reading books; and he produced a book which has astonished the linguists, the eloquent and ready speakers, and subjugated to him the necks of the Arab nation. He said on behalf of the Most High God: "Say 'Bring ten Sūrahs like it devised; and call upon whom ye can beside God, if ye do tell the truth.'"[2] And he said: "Then bring a Sūrah like it, and call your witnesses other than God, if ye tell truth."[3] There was no one left in the nation to murmur and to speak, but all befriended him, submitted, and yielded.

The learned men among the protected cults object that the Prophet—peace be with him—should have been an unlettered man, because God does not spare His prophets the knowledge of writing, this knowledge being the best He could bestow upon them, and the least of His secrets and miracles He could reveal to them. The answer to this objection is that the Most High God has qualified each one of them with what He pleased. Some of them were excellent speakers, such as David; and some of them were lispers and stammerers, such as

[1] A gentilic of *Abṭaḥ*, a clan of the tribe of Ḳuraish (*Hish.* i. 163); and one of the names of the Prophet.

[2] Ḳur. xi. 16.

[3] Ḳur. ii. 21.

Moses. Some of them gave life to the dead and rent asunder the sea, and made springs of water jet out of rocks, to the exclusion of others. Some of them were literary men and writers, such as Solomon; and some were unlettered, such as David, who said in his Psalter: "Because I did not know how to write;"[1] this is not a dishonour to him, as it is not a dishonour to Christ not to have been a dexterous spearer,[2] a skilled archer, a surveyor, an architect. And as it is not considered a dishonour for Moses not to have had fluency and eloquence of speech, or not to have walked on the air, or not to have healed a blind man and a leper, and as it is not considered a dishonour for David and others—peace be with them—that God did not take them up to heaven, in the way that He did for others, it is not permissible to say that God was grudging towards this and that prophet in what He had granted to this and that prophet. He who says this is insolent and a rebel.

Do we not see that Simon Cephas, Matthew, and Luke, disciples of Christ—peace be with them—have not been traduced because they did not reach the measure of Paul in eloquence and rhetoric? Likewise, it is not a dishonour to the Prophet—may God bless and save him—to have been an unlettered man, like David. On the contrary, God has made of this point a resplendent miracle and an argument against the men of his nation who disbelieved in him; because it became evident to the Muslim communities and to the members of the protected cults that he had not produced the Ḳur'ān as an outcome of literary eloquence or earthly wisdom.

He was—peace be with him—brief, concise, and slow in his speech, and he blamed the loquacious and talkative. It has come to our knowledge that 'Āyeshah—may God be pleased with her—would say: "The Prophet—may God bless and save him—did not continue his speech

[1] Ps. lxxi. 15 (Peshiṭta Version).

[2] Lit. "Spear-player," a title of three poets mentioned in *Tāj.* (s.v.).

uninterruptedly, as you do; his speech was concisely cut short, and you display yours ceaselessly."[1] He went one day to speak, but was embarrassed, and became silent; then he said: "This difficulty in speaking fluently affects sometimes the prophets." And he—peace be with him—heard somebody using pompous verbosity of speech, and articulating with affectation, and he silenced him;[2] then he went and said to those who were present: "Be natural in your speech, and let Satan fascinate you not; verily, people among you whom I most love, and who will be the nearest to me in the day of Resurrection, are those who have the best work; and people among you whom I most hate, and who will be the remotest from me in the day of Resurrection, are those who have the worst work; verily, I do hate the chatterers, the pretentious, and those who indulge in grandiloquence."

Therefore, the question of his being unlettered, for which he has been blamed by the men of the protected cults, is not a dishonour nor a discredit to him; on the contrary, it is a proof and an enlightening argument in his favour. If a literary and eloquent man had brought forth such a book as that I have described it would have been a miracle; what would then be the case if its author were a man of the desert, and unlettered? This is a clear proof that God has made him pronounce it, and that the Holy Spirit has assisted and directed him in it.

[1] Cf. I.S. i. ii. 97. *Buk.* iv. 200.

[2] Cf. *Musn.* ii. 94.

X.

CHAPTER VII.

THE VICTORY OF THE PROPHET—MAY GOD BLESS AND SAVE HIM—IS A MARK OF PROPHETIC OFFICE.

Among the miracles of the Prophet—peace be with him—is his victory, which all Muslims have used as an argument. I believed formerly, as other Christians believe, that victory was a point common to all nations, and that what was common was not a sign of prophetic office. When I awoke from the intoxication of error, and arose from the slumber of indecision, and got rid of the aberration of tradition, I knew then that the question was not as they believed. Because the Prophet—may God bless and save him—came out an orphan, unique, and poor, as the Most High God said: "Did He not find thee an orphan, and give thee shelter? And find thee erring, and guide thee? And find thee poor with a family, and nourish thee?"[1] And he called all the Arabs and all the nations to the belief in the Most High God, while people were shooting at him from one bow, sneering at him, and stirred against him; this did not deter him, nor did it discourage him, but he preached his religion without flinching, and went forward towards what God had ordered him, without shrinking. When he noticed that they were rejecting his order, thinking evil of him, and not entering willingly into the religion and the grace of God, he made them enter into it by force; his claim then triumphed, and the Arabs one and all submitted to him; next, miracles and prophecies succeeded one another among them, and the new religion

[1] Ḳur. xciii. 6-8.

became dear to them, and truth resplendent; then, after their hate and their enmity, their love and attachment to him reached what the adversaries see and hear.

Who has ever claimed such a victory, in the name of God, since the creation of the world by God? a victory comprising conditions and good qualities such as call to the Creator of heaven and earth, abstraction from this world, encouragement for the world to come, prevention from associating other gods and helpers with God and from committing iniquity and impurity? a victory which was realised in such a decisive and unquestionable way, in all the countries and regions of the earth, on sea and land, from the extreme Sūs[1] to the deserts of Turkestan and Tibet, by means of devotees and deeply pious leaders, and by proclamations in the name of the God of Abraham, Ishmael, Isaac, Jacob, and the rest of the prophets? His disciples were distinguished by contempt of the world, abstinence from its possessions and cares, and self-denial in every pleasure and passion; and were satisfied with food strictly sufficient for the maintenance of the body; and had such orders for equality of asseveration and right in judicial decisions, that if a believing Muslim had killed a member of protected cults, an unbeliever, the Muslim would have to be killed, as retaliation and justice;[2] we know with certainty that such a victory undoubtedly takes the place of a sign of prophetic office.

As to the victories of other nations, which they oppose to us, if they had relinquished the passions which blind and deafen, and discerned their motives, they would have known that the victory of Alexander, of Ardāshīr, son of Bābak, and of others was not in God, nor for God, nor for His prophets, but its aim was solely fame, power, and reputation, while the victors were either Atheists,[3] or Dualists, or Pagans; and this cannot

[1] In Morocco (*Yāḳūt*, iii. 189).

[2] This is against the doctrine of the *Musn.* ii. 178, 180. The author's view is shared by Abu Ḥanīfah.

[3] In Arabic *Dahrī*, i.e. believing in the eternity of matter.

be compared with the dignity and sublimity of the victory of Islām. To this victory there is another sufficient and decisive evidence, viz. it cannot fail to have emanated either from God or from Satan; if they confess that it is from God, Islām is then true, and they ought to accept it and embrace it; and if they pretend that it is from Satan, Satan would then be in agreement and not in disagreement with God and His prophets, obedient and not rebellious, since he would have helped the man who had called to the One and Eternal God, and promoted the religion of the man who had ordered fasting and prayer, prohibited fornication, unbelief, immorality, and iniquity, and made the exaltation and glorification of God his rallying-cry in fighting, his vanguard in attacking, and his armour in charging and thrusting. He who believes that Satan would help to make such a religion prevail and be maintained has indeed a good opinion of him, speaks well of him, and contradicts what God and His prophets have said about him. How can Satan help a man who calls to such a religion as this in which his roots are pulled up, his chances cut off, and his followers and disciples utterly destroyed?

Some wicked people thought the same thing of the Messiah—peace be with Him—and the Rabbis of the Jews said of Him: "This one drives out demons by means of the prince of the demons." But the Christ said to them: "Every kingdom which is divided against itself shall perish, and shall not stand, and every city in which there is disunion and disagreement shall not last, and shall not be firm; if it is Satan who casts out Satan, how then can his kingdom and his might last?"[1] And the Jews were put to shame.

This is our argument against those who say of the Prophet—may God bless and save him—what the Jews said of the Messiah—peace be with Him. Among what the Prophet—peace be with him—related on behalf of

[1] Matt. xii. 24-26.

God about Satan is the following saying: "Ay, the partisans of Satan, they are the losers."[1] And he said: "Verily the devil is to you a foe, so take him as a foe; he only calls his partisans to be the fellows of the blaze."[2] And he said: "Go forth therefrom, for, verily, thou art pelted, and, verily, upon thee is my curse unto the day of judgment."[3] And he said: "I will surely fill hell with thee and with those who follow thee amongst them all together."[4] And he said: "O ye who believe, follow not the traces of Satan."[5] And he said: "I seek refuge in the Lord of men, the King of men, the God of men, from the evil of the Whisperer who slinks off."[6] And the Prophet—peace be with him—ordered us to take refuge in God from him, in every prayer and at every opportune moment by saying: "I take refuge in the Hearer and the Knower, from the stoned Satan."[7]

If Satan helps the man who curses him and unveils his wickedness to the world, we shall not be secure against the fact that all the religions which appeared in the name of a Unique God might have been in agreement with Satan, and from him. All the nations agree that Satan enjoins association of other gods with God, and worship of idols and fire; that he favours adultery, fornication, and treachery, which are the objects of his desire and his suggestions; that he is an enemy of God, and an enemy of His prophets who command the contrary of all this. Since God cannot be of the followers of Satan, and Satan cannot be of the followers of God, the victory of the Prophet is then from God and not from someone else.

[1] Ḳur. lviii. 20.
[2] Ḳur. xxxv. 6.
[3] Ḳur. xxxviii. 78-79.
[4] Ḳur. xxxviii. 85.
[5] Ḳur. xxiv. 21.
[6] Ḳur. cxiv. 1-4.
[7] This sentence is not found in the Ḳur'ān; it is perhaps quoted from a traditional saying.

XI.

CHAPTER VIII.

THOSE WHO CALLED TO HIS RELIGION AND WITNESSED THE TRUTH OF HIS CAUSE WERE MOST HONEST AND RIGHTEOUS MEN.

Some people have attributed forgery and falsehood to the disciples of the Prophet—may God bless and save him—but because they have traduced them, they have sinned, and because they have deviated from their right path, they have gone astray. I shall narrate from their virtues, their asceticism, and their piety some facts that would cause such people to think well of them and cease their disparagement.

XII.

ASCETICISM OF ABU BAKR—MAY GOD BE PLEASED WITH HIM.

The first one is Abu Bakr—may God be pleased with him. His detachment from the world, his contempt of it, and his keeping away from it reached such a pitch, that when he was called to the Caliphate, which is the most exalted office in the world for dignity and the greatest for honour, the one which carries with it in the highest degree might, majesty, power, pleasure, and security, he refused and rejected it, until it was forced upon him. Some days after his election he turned to the people, crying in a loud voice: "Is there anybody to cancel it? Is there anybody to cancel it?" When nobody answered him, he addressed the people, saying: "My election was a surprise; I only accepted it because I feared divisions; by God, I did not covet it, either in day or in night, nor did I ask it from God, either secretly or openly; I have no pleasure in it nor capacity for it."[1] Has anyone heard of a man more noble than this, more humble and modest, and more lofty in care for heavenly things?

His self-restraint and his scrupulousness reached such a point that he fixed for himself a monthly allowance of sixty *dirhams*[2] from the fund of the Muslims. It has been said that he asked that this stipend should be taken from him and paid back to the fund of the Muslims in order that he might spend from his own earnings, as others did; this the Muslims refused, and he said to them: "Then I return your Caliphate to you; by God, I shall not hold it except on this condition;" then they agreed.—It has come to our knowledge that he—may God be pleased with him—has been seen, some days after he had become Caliph, offering his shirt to be sold by auction.—It has been said to him in his illness: "We will call a physician for thee;" and he answered: "The physician saw me." They said "And what did he tell thee?" And he said "He told me that God does what pleases Him."[3] When his illness became more severe, he said "Where is your physician? Let him divert it if he is right; by the One who has glorified the Father of al-Ḳāsim,[4] there is no soul in the earth that I would wish to see pass away in preference to my soul, not even the soul of this fragile fly; do you know why?" They said "No;" and he said "By God, because I fear that shortcomings should interpose between me and Islām."

At the time of his death he declared to 'Umar ibnul-Khaṭṭāb—may God be pleased with him—saying "O 'Umar, if thou fulfillest my recommendation, thou wilt meet with no accident more profitable than death, with

[1] Cf. Suyūṭi, 70 (edit. Jarret).
[2] I.S. iii. i. 132 says 6000 *dirhams*.
[3] Cf. Suyūṭi, 82.
[4] I.e. the Prophet Muḥammad.

which in any case thou wilt surely meet; but if thou neglectest my recommendation, there will be no accident with which thou mayest meet worse than this same death, which thou canst not avoid." When death was near, he declared to 'Umar—may God be pleased with both of them—saying "I have acquired nothing from the fund of the Muslims but this young camel on which I laid the water which I and others drank, and this maid-servant who served me and you, and this mantle." Then he spurned the latter with his foot and said "And I have given back all that, and I am well and happy."[1]

His piety and justice reached such a point that when two men came quarrelling before him, the one letting not the other finish his evidence, Abu Bakr restrained him several times from that, but he did not desist; then Abu Bakr lifted up his staff, and the man, in parrying it with his hand, touched its handle, which broke off; whereupon he went away. Abu Bakr—may God be pleased with him—was much afflicted, and said to 'Umar "Would that I had never accepted this charge; and no one deceived me in it but thee." And 'Umar said "By God, this charge is more necessary to thee than thy own ear; by God, we must strike now with sticks, now with swords." Then he rose up in the company of 'Umar, and went to the house of that man; and Abu Bakr presented the staff to him, and knelt down before him, and said to him: "O man, retaliate; it is more pleasing to me that this should be speedily done." The man refused, saying "I was on the point of coming to thee to ask thee to forgive me, because I irritated thee." And 'Umar said to the man "Do what he has asked, and absolve him." And the man said "O Caliph of the Apostle of God, thou art absolved; may God forgive thee." Then Abu Bakr stood up, saying "May God forgive thee as thou hast forgiven me, and may He pardon thee as thou hast pardoned me."

[1] Cf. I.S. iii. i. 136 seqq.

And he—may God be pleased with him—delivered a speech and said "I have assumed government over you, while I am not the best of you. If I am right, help me, and if I fail, strengthen me; he that is weak among you is strong before me, until I have rendered justice to him; and he that is strong among you is weak before me, until I have extorted justice from him; sincerity is an obligation, and deceit is a treason; as long as I obey God, obey me; but if I rebel against Him, I have no right to be obeyed by you."[1]

To a man with such detachment from the world when possessing it, and to him who spoke in such a way about the Caliphate which was imposed upon him, why should we attribute acceptance and utterance of falsehood?

[1] Cf. I.S. iii. i. 129. *Ṭab.* 1, 4, 1829, and 1845-6. *Suyūṭi*, 69.

XIII.

ASCETICISM OF 'UMAR IBNUL-KHAṬṬĀB — MAY GOD'S GRACE AND PLEASURE BE WITH HIM.

There is nothing in the world higher than the Caliphate, and nothing lower than a mere pittance. Therefore, if the Caliphate comes to a man freely and spontaneously, and he abstains from it, and is content with his mere subsistence from it, and satisfied with nakedness and poverty, while spreading pebbles under him as a mattress, and using his arm as a pillow, and refraining his soul from every passion and pleasure, and rejecting and despising the treasures of Chosrau hidden for thousands of years when brought to him, and not stretching his hand to a *dirham*, nor a *dīnār*, nor a pearl, nor a precious stone, nor a rich garment, nor a jewel, nor a male-servant, nor a slave-girl from them, who in the earth is more pious, more modest, and more austere than he?

When he had to dispatch an army, he would say: "O men, I owe you what I have engaged myself to do the day I assumed government over you: that I should not take a *dirham* from your possessions without paying for it; and if it comes to me, that I should not spend it except in the right way; that I should not detain you long, when you have been dispatched; that I should not impose upon you a task beyond your power; and that I should be the father of your family until you come back." He would repair to the houses of wives whose husbands were absent, and greet them, and being the Commander of the Faithful, buy himself their necessary things, and bring them the letters of their husbands and dispatch their letters to them.

It is related that seeing a wife whose husband was absent carrying a jar, 'Umar—may God be pleased with him—took the jar from her and carried it on his head until he reached her house.—He met an old Christian begging and saying "O my God, judge between me and the Muslims; they have taken tribute from me when I was young, and they have betrayed me when I became old." And 'Umar said: "Here is 'Umar at thy service." Then he went with haste, filled a sack with flour, and called a porter to carry it; then he said to him "No, I would rather carry it myself;" and he carried it on his head, and brought it to the old man with some money that he gave him; and he granted him a monthly allowance for his food.

A basket of sweets had been sent to him, and he said: "Has something like it been sent to all the Muslims?" They answered "No." And he said: "There is no need for me to have an enjoyment or a food which is not common to all the Muslims;" and he ordered that it should be taken away.—It has been said to him at the time of his illness "We will bring thee a physician;" and he said: "If my recovery depended on an anointment of my ear, I would not have anointed it; how good is my Lord to whom I am going!"—The inhabitants of Damascus observed how he alighted from his camel, led it, reached a river, sat down, took off his sandals with his own hands, and crossed the river; and they said: "We have not seen a King in asceticism except this."

It is related that 'Ali ibn Abu Ṭālib—may God be pleased with him—was once working in a garden that he had, and he heard a loud voice. And Ḥasan, son of 'Ali—peace be with both of them—said: "Father, come up, and thou wilt see a wonder." It was 'Umar running after a camel of the alms-fund which had bolted; and he was dripping with sweat. And 'Ali—may God be pleased with him—said, "This is the quick and clever son of

Ḥantamah,[1] gentle without being weak, and firm without being severe."

When Hormizān, King of Ahwāz, was brought before him, arrayed in his gorgeous garments, he (Hormizān) said to the crowd who were looking with amazement at him: "Where is the Commander of the Faithful?" They answered: "He is that man who is asleep." He said: "Where are his chamberlains?" They answered: "He has no chamberlains." He said: "Where is his body-guard?" They answered: "He is the body-guard of himself." He said: "Where are his throne and his bolster?" They answered: "His throne is the ground and earth, his mattress is the pebbles, and his bolster is his hand." And he said to them: "It is by this that you have overcome us. You have made light of life and the world, and we have loved both of them."

When the treasures and the precious stones of Chosrau were brought to him and poured out in the mosque, he showed sorrow; and it was said to him: "O Commander of the Faithful, it is a day of joy;" and he said: "No people have had such a conquest without having displayed their strength among themselves." He then sat down and began to divide the booty with the palm of his hand. His son was sitting aloof like a sheep with a broken leg.[2] When he noticed that his father was not giving him anything, he said: "O father, it seems that thou dost not believe that I have a right to this booty." 'Umar answered: "Yes, my boy; but I fear that my palm should become broader for thee." One of those who were present said: "I will give him what thy palm has contained for me, and fill thy palm afresh for me." And he did that.—And his little daughter took a *dirham* from the booty; he shouted at her, but she did not throw it.

[1] Mother of 'Umar and daughter of Hāshim, son of Mughīrah (*Ṭab.* I, 5, 27-28).

[2] Proverb meaning "He was quiet and distressed."

And 'Umar—may God be pleased with him—rose and went to her; and the child put it in her mouth; but he did not cease to press her throat until she ejected it.—A man gave him two garments, but he sold them, and with their price he bought five slaves whom he manumitted, saying: "The man who prefers two coats to the emancipation of these is feeble-minded."

XIV.

ASCETICISM OF 'ALI IBN ABU ṬĀLIB[1]—MAY GOD BE PLEASED WITH HIM.

It is said that some days after 'Ali ibn Abu Ṭālib—may God honour him—was made Caliph, he was seen offering his sword to be sold by auction, while saying: "Had we supper for one night, we would not have sold it," and he was of all men the one who most needed it, but necessity compelled him to sell it; and he had every year much money from the corn of a real estate that he possessed.—He would empty every day the house of the public treasury, sprinkle it with water, and sleep in it, saying: "O gold, beguile other than me; the ground has become empty for thee, and thou mayst be white or yellow."[2]

It is told that at night he had a torn and worn out mantle over him. The maid put on him and his family a mantle from the mantles of the alms-fund. He disliked its soft nap, and said "What is this?" She answered "It is a mantle from the alms-fund;" and he threw it away from himself and said: "You have made us feel the cold for the rest of the night."—Once when he was in his house a man called him; he went out to him with haste, saying "Here I am at your service!"

[1] Since a special chapter is devoted to 'Ali by a courtier of Mutawakkil, it seems that there is some exaggeration in the matter of the hatred which some Muslim historians attribute to Mutawakkil against the memory of 'Ali.

[2] Cf. *Tāj*. iii. 335.

XV.

ASCETICISM OF 'UMAR IBN 'ABDUL-'AZĪZ, AND OF 'ABDALLAH IBN 'UMAR IBNUL-KHAṬṬĀB, AND OF SOME OTHER PIOUS MUSLIMS—MAY GOD BE PLEASED WITH ALL OF THEM.

IF somebody says that the above men were accustomed to poverty, and that the only proper thing for them to do was what they did, the answer is that it generally happens that a man accustomed to poverty becomes extravagant in pleasures when coming to a condition of wealth, and takes from it the opportunity of doing what had escaped him in his early days. So, Mu'āwiah, and his son Yazīd, and the Umayyad Caliphs who succeeded them, lived in pleasure and had their satisfaction in everything associated with food, drink, dresses, perfumes, and passion. In their government two goats did not butt each other,[1] and there were not two men to oppose them. An exception is to be made in the case of Walīd ibn Yazīd ibn 'Abdul-Malik, who having completely withdrawn the veil of shame, thrown modesty away and neglected his charge, was beleaguered, and met with the decreed fate.[2]

But this 'Umar ibn 'Abdul-Azīz—may God's grace be with him—although preceded by many luxurious brothers of the world such as those we have mentioned, did not indulge in anything of the kind they had done. His asceticism and his contemptuousness for the world reached such a pitch that after having been the most handsome and the best scented man of all his contemporaries, the most elegant and graceful in attire, he mounted the pulpit after he had been made Caliph, and

[1] i.e. nobody showed them the slightest opposition.

[2] He was killed.

said: "By God, I did not desire this office at all, nor did I ask it from God secretly or openly; if there is one who does not want me, now is his time." He confirmed this saying by the following fact: One of the steps in the stairs of his house was demolished; a relative of his restored it. But 'Umar—may God be pleased with him—said: "Praise be to God! It seems that the one who did this had envied me for the fact that I would leave the world without having put one brick upon another." Then he ordered that it should be demolished.

The maid brought him hot water on a cold day. He said to her: "Wherefrom obtainedst thou this?" She answered: "We have heated it where the food of the Muslims is cooked." And he said: "Hadst thou not brought it by ignorance, thou wouldst not have served me any more; give them the price of the wood."—His servant bought him a garment for ten *dirhams;* but he said: "This is too soft, I want one of a lower quality." And the servant said: "Before his Caliphate I bought him a garment of embroidered silk for seven hundred *dīnārs*, and he said that he wanted one of a better quality." He was once informed that the Umayyads were grieved at the manner he used to remove abuses, and he said "I wish God had removed all abuses for me, because whenever I remove an abuse a bit is cut off my body, but at the leaving of my soul I shall remove the last abuse."[1] —And he said: "I did not lie, ever since I had my reason; a lie dishonours the man who utters it."

The prefect of Ḥimṣ wrote to him requesting an increase of allowance for the expenses of his paper and of his lamp-oil, and asking his permission to restore the ramparts of the city; and he wrote to him: "Make thy

[1] The energy displayed by this Caliph for the removal of abuses is best illustrated by the following saying reported by *Suyūṭī* (p. 361): "The Caliphs are but three—Abu Bakr for his waging war on the apostates, 'Umar b. 'Abdul-'Azīz for his removal of abuses, and Mutawakkil for his revival of traditional doctrine."

pen thinner, and render thy speech concise in combining two needs in one; as to the lamp-oil, my recommendation is that thou shouldst go in a dark night to the mosque without light; as to the ramparts of the city, thou shouldst fortify thy city in justice, and purify its streets from iniquity."

The prefect of 'Irāḳ wrote to him that a great fortune was gathered in the public treasury; and he enjoined him to increase with it the stipends of the Muslims, for their welfare and the welfare of their children. The prefect wrote to him that he has done so, and much fortune was left; and he enjoined him to marry young men to young women. The prefect wrote to him that he has done it, and much fortune was still left; and he answered him that he should encourage the members of protected cults to build houses, and to lend them money in advance, because 'Umar and the family of 'Umar were in no need of anything from it.[1]

It has come to our knowledge that 'Abdallah ibn 'Umar ibnul-Khaṭṭāb—may God's mercy be with both of them—liked grapes in his illness; his people found him a bunch, and bought it for one *dīnār*. A man came asking for grapes, and he ordered that it should be given to him; and they went and bought it back from the man, and returned it to him. Another man came asking for grapes, and again he gave it to him, and refused to taste it.

It has come also to our knowledge, that when Rabī' ibn Khaitham[2]—may God's grace be with him—became ill and was asked if he would call a physician. He answered: "I first wanted that, but then I abstained from it and said 'Where are 'Ād, Thamūd, and Ḳārūn? There is much to be said about them. There were physicians among them, but none of the attendants or those attended

[1] This story is related by I.S. iii. i. 215 of the Caliph 'Umar b. Khaṭṭāb.

[2] A man with this name occurs in *Ṭab.* (3, 4, 2553) as Khuthaim. Cf. the remark of Flügel (p. 98) on the text of the *Fihrist* (p. 225).

to was left; what is then the meaning of a physician when nothing can stop death?'"

A man from Syria, who had become governor of Baṣrah, used to deceive the readers of the Ḳur'ān in enticing them into accepting stipends and gifts from him. He related that to an ascetic woman; and she said to him: "O Corruptor of the Readers! by God, I am ashamed to ask an earthly thing from the Possessor of the earth, how could I then ask it from a poor servant like myself?"

One of the Hāshimite governors of Kūfah heard of much asceticism and self-abnegation concerning a devotee, and sent him much money; but the man refused to accept it. The Hāshimite believed that he was one of those who hated the Hāshimites' coming into power, and believed their money to be illicit; and he wanted to punish him. This reached the ears of the man, who stood up, performed many *rak'ahs*, and said: "O Lord, they have made me love that from which Thou hast held me back, and they have wanted me to do what Thou hast forbidden me to do; take me then to Thee." And they found him dead in his hut.

One of the Caliphs made his pilgrimage, and came to an ascetic of Maccah, who, however, did not lift up his head to look at him. He offered him much money to distribute among people he knew, but the ascetic refused to accept it. He asked him to advise him, and the ascetic said: "Fear God in the Muslim affairs, the settlement of which He has confided to thee, and be content with the Kur'ān as guide and teacher."

Such is the asceticism of several kings, princes, and men of piety in the Muslim community, who, among the kings of the earth and the nations of the prophets, have no one comparable and similar to them since the creation of the world. Falsehood and lies are not attributed to men of this kind; indeed, the earth embraced them, and they fled from it; it came to them with the beautiful things found on its surface, but they turned their backs to it; it threw open to them the precious minerals of its interior[1] and its hidden treasures; it laid at their feet its most subtle traps and its most alluring baits and charms, but they did not come near them, and were satisfied with tatters and rags and with unpalatable and coarse food. Before their conversion to Islām, they were men of power, pride, wealth, cattle, flocks, property, and possessions. I say this in the truth outside which I do not love anything, for the sake of which I uphold every saying, and outside which I have no hope for any success. If lies and falsehood may be ascribed to men who endured so much and triumphed so brilliantly over the world, no one will be exempt from this suspicion and accusation.

The disciples of Moses and of Christ—peace be with them—were pious and upright; no one is ashamed of truth, which must be set above everything. But if men comparable to those we have mentioned are suspected, *a fortiori* we may suspect a man who did not reach the degree of their asceticism, and was not tested with the like of their hardships and the process of their refinement. If we must accept the sayings and trust the narrative of the disciples of Moses and Christ—peace be with them—who left a net, or abandoned an advantageous affair, or renounced a business, or a field, *a fortiori* we must trust a man who owned all the Caliphate, but deemed it more despicable than spittle in the river or dung in the sea.[2]

If somebody advances the statement: "Your masters endured what you have mentioned for the sake of power and dignity," we will rebut it with a similar statement and say: "This is the case also with your masters, because when they moved from a low and mean estate to that in which people obeyed them and sought to be blessed by them, and wealthy and influential men gathered round them, and had effective orders for men

[1] *Lit.*, "Liver."

[2] Proverb meaning something low, small, and despicable.

and money—their soul desired dignity, for the sake of which they endured hardship and privation." You know what Simon Cephas did to a man who had sold his estate and brought him its price in order to ingratiate himself with him by means of it; his reward with him was that he was irritated against him, and asked God to kill him at once with his wife, because the poor man had not brought him all the price, but had kept back something for himself and his wife.[1] One is loth to impute avarice to the disciples of Christ; do not impute it then to the disciples of Muḥammad—peace be with him.

If they say "Although your masters were themselves honest and pious, yet we suspect them because their testimony was for their cousin and for the sake of attracting people to his religion," we will answer "This was also the case with your masters; since the only witnesses of Moses and Christ were their cousins."

If they say "What need have we of the testimony of our co-religionists when your Prophet believes in our prophets?" we will say "What would you say then about the man who had accepted the claims of your prophets before the appearance of the Prophet—may God bless and save him?" Was he right or wrong? Was he sound-minded or feeble-minded? Further, between the description of the Christ in whom the Muslims believe and your Christ there is a great gap; the Christians say that He is eternal, but with us He is not eternal; they relate that He is Creator, but with us He is created; they pretend that He was killed, but with us He is living. These are contradictory and not synonymous terms.

Moreover, there is an obligation on the part of all men towards God to seek after truth and to follow it in all ages; and there is an obligation on the part of God—may His memory be exalted—towards men, to confirm truth, to make it prevail, and to destroy the arguments of those who waver in its acceptance. We do not doubt

[1] Acts v. 1 seq.

that many nations surrounding Egypt and Syria had heard, before the appearance of Muḥammad—may God bless and save him—the history of Moses and that of the rest of the prophets, and their souls were longing for it as well as for the history of Christ, and were seeking information about them from those they happened to meet; now were those people obliged to accept what they were hearing concerning those prophets and to believe in it, or not? If you do not declare its acceptance as necessary, you will disbelieve in every prophet; and if you declare it to be necessary, we will ask "Why should it be necessary when those who announced it and bore witness to it were either Jews or Christians, and he who accepts the saying of his co-religionists and is deceived by it, according to your opinion contradicts truth and inclines to inaccuracy and falsehood, because he has accepted about his prophets the statements of their co-religionists and their cousins who did not possess either miracles or evidence. If the acceptance of such statements was obligatory for those nations, before the Prophet Muḥammad—may God bless and save him—bore witness to them, the acceptance, therefore, of the statements of the companions of the Prophet—may God bless and save him—concerning their master is likewise obligatory; the more so, that the prophets had borne witness to him, described his origin and his time, and mentioned, for the verification of their statements, what the Muslims only can claim. If the Jews set forth, with ignorance and pride, a claim to those prophecies which I will relate, what will the Christians say who testify that God has destroyed the Jews, erased their religion from the register of the earth, and declared that He will not have mercy on them, nor will He cancel any of their lapses, nor will He accept from them any atonement or ransom, unless they divert from Judaism and disavow their connection with it?

XVI.

CHAPTER IX.

IF THE PROPHET—MAY GOD BLESS AND SAVE HIM—HAD NOT APPEARED, THE PROPHECIES OF THE PROPHETS ABOUT ISHMAEL—PEACE BE WITH HIM—AND ABOUT THE PROPHET—PEACE BE WITH HIM—WHO IS THE LAST OF THE PROPHETS, WOULD HAVE NECESSARILY BECOME WITHOUT OBJECT.

THE Most High God does not contradict His promise, nor does He belie His words and disappoint the man who puts his trust in Him. He had announced to Abraham—peace be with him—and Hagar—God's mercy be with her—clear and joyful messages, which we do not see fulfilled and realised except by the appearance of the Prophet—may God bless and save him. Indeed, to Hagar messages have been announced such as no wife of ancient men can claim the like of them, after the pure and the virgin Mary, mother of the Christ—peace be with him. Moreover, to Mary—peace be with her—the Christ was announced once only, while to Hagar Ishmael was announced twice; and to his father—peace be with him—he was announced several times. God willing, I will explain this in its due place.

What the Most High God revealed to Abraham—peace be with him—exclusively about Ishmael, is His saying through Moses—peace be with him—in the tenth chapter of the first Book of the Torah. God said there to Abraham—peace be with him—"I have heard (thy prayer)[1] about Ishmael; I have blessed him, increased him, and magnified him exceedingly: twelve princes

[1] In the Biblical quotations of the following pages the words between parentheses are missing in the Syriac Version.

shall he beget, and I will make him a great nation."[1] This is in the version of Marcus, the translator (*tarjamān*); but in the Torah, translated by seventy-two Jewish priests, it is said "He will beget twelve nations."[2] No promises and no announcements about anyone could be greater than the saying of the Most High God: "I have blessed him, increased him, and multiplied him exceedingly." Less than this coming from the Most High God is great, and not so much as this is sublime, because the measure that God considers as considerable and exceedingly great, there is no measure greater than it. This is a rebuke and a rebuff to that rude and impudent man who found fault with Ishmael and derided him, because God said about him: "He will be a wild ass of men." I will explain it in this chapter as a rebuff against that blockhead and dolt.[3]

Moses—peace be with him—had already prophesied with a prophecy similar to this in the ninth chapter of the first Book, saying that when Hagar fled from Sarah, the angel of God appeared to her and said: "O Hagar, Sarai's maid, whence comest thou, and where art thou going?" (Hagar answering him) said: "I flee from my mistress Sarai." The angel of the Lord said unto her "Return to thy mistress and submit to her; because I will multiply (thy posterity and) thy seed, that it shall not be numbered for multitude,[4] and behold thou shalt be with child, and shalt bear a son, and shalt call his name Ishmael, because God hath heard (thy affliction) and thy humility; and he will be a wild ass of men, and his hand

[1] Genes. xvii. 20.
[2] Sept., δώδεκα ἔθνη γεννήσει.

[3] Al-Kindi said to his opponent with reference to an unnamed man: "Including a person whom thou knowest and whose name I should tremble to write," *Apology*, p. 89 (edit. Muir). The person alluded to by the Christian apologist seems to have been Ishmael, the wild ass. The word *'air* is used in many derisive senses, and in Mesopotamia it means in our days "pudenda hominis."

[4] The Arabic lacks "And the angel of the Lord said to her" found in Syriac.

will be over all, and the hand of all (stretched) to him,[1] and his abode shall be on all his brother's frontiers."[2] This is the second announcement uttered face to face by the angel to Hagar—peace be with her—on behalf of the Most High God; and he told her that God would make her son's hand the higher, and the hand of all others the lower with regard to him. We have not seen that this point of the prophecy of Moses—peace be with him—was fulfilled and realised, except after the appearance of the Prophet Muḥammad—may God bless and save him.

And Moses said, in the thirteenth chapter of the first Book, that God said to Abraham—peace be with him—"And also of the son of thy bondwoman will I make a great nation, because he is from thy seed."[3] This is the third prophecy about Ishmael—peace be with him. After this saying, Moses said "And when Abraham rose up in the morning (he took out of his habitation Hagar and his child, in conformity to the wish of Sarah, and went to where God had ordered him about her; and he gave her food and provisions, and put the child on her shoulder, and sent her away on her journey. And Hagar departed)[4] and wandered in the wilderness (called) Beersheba; and her water was spent;[5] and she cast the child under one of the shrubs, and went off[6] at a distance of a bow-shot[7] in order that she[8] might not see the death of her son. And for that she was weeping and grieved. And God heard the voice of the lad, and the angel of God called to

[1] i.e. soliciting favour from him. These words explain the meaning of "a higher and a lower hand" of the following lines. The higher or upper hand is that which gives, and the lower hand is that which receives. A saying to this effect on the part of the Prophet is reported by Bukhāri and Muslim. See also Ḳasṭallāni's *Irshād* iii 30-32, and Ibn Ḥanbal's *Musn.* ii. 67.

[2] Genes. xvi. 8-13.

[3] Genes. xxi. 13.

[4] All this is somewhat paraphrastic.

[5] The Syriac adds "from the water skin."

[6] Syr. adds "against (him)."

[7] Syr. adds "because she said."

[8] Syr. "I."

Hagar out of heaven, and said 'What aileth thee, Hagar? Let thy heart rejoice, for God hath heard the voice of the lad;[1] arise, lift him up, and take hold of him, for (God) will make him a great nation.' And God opened her eyes, and behold![2] a well of water; and she crawled and filled the bottle (from it), and gave the lad drink from it. And God was with her and with the lad[3] until he grew; and his abode was in the wilderness of Paran, and he applied himself to learn archery."[4]

This prophecy of Moses—peace be with him—about Ishmael and his mother Hagar is similar to the saying of the angel Gabriel to the virgin Mary: "Our Lord is with thee, O blessed among women."[5] The Christians have been deluded by this saying, and have said that God was dwelling in her, because Gabriel said to her "Our Lord is with thee;" but Moses—peace be with him—said the same thing about Hagar, that "God was with her and with the lad until he grew."

These are four messages exclusively about Ishmael—peace be with him. Two of them came down to Abraham and two to Hagar. Let that stupid and feeble-minded man find us messages more numerous, more resplendent and genuine than these from the Most High God, which have followed one another over parents for the sake of their child, since the beginning of the world.

The messages delivered by God to Abraham concerning all his posterity and children are also two; one of them is the saying of the Most High God to Abraham, when he offered his son for sacrifice: "Because thou hast done this deed,[6] and hast not withheld thy son, thine only son, by myself do I swear that I will bless thee, I will multiply thy posterity (and I will make them) as the number of the stars of the heaven, and as the sand of the

[1] Syr. adds "where he is."
[2] Syr. "and she saw."
[3] The translator misunderstood the Syriac corroborative which only means "with the lad."
[4] Genes. xxi. 14-21.
[5] Luk. i. 28.
[6] Syr. "Order, message."

sea shores; and thy children shall inherit the countries of their enemies; and in them[1] shall all the nations of the earth be blessed."[2] The Torah says, too: "Abraham said 'Behold I am dying, and I have no child, and no successor; and my heir is my servant,[3] and one born in my house.' Then the Lord said to him 'This shall not be thine heir;[4] but he[5] that shall come out of thine own loins shall be thine heir. Get out[6] and look toward the stars of heaven; if thou art able to number them, thou shalt number also thy children.'"[7]

The first four prophecies are exclusively about Ishmael, and Ishmael has, too, a share with Isaac and his other brethren in the last two; these make six peremptory prophecies and messages about him. In spite of this, that rude Garmecite,[8] wicked and ignorant, pretends that Ishmael is not counted among the children of Abraham—peace be with him. The above words were realised and fulfilled by the appearance of the Prophet—may God bless and save him. Prior to that, all Christians and Jews knew that the children of Abraham, known by his name, and related to him,[9] did not cease to be among various nations of the earth. A company of them were in Egypt as slaves to Pharaohs and to Copts, treated rudely and oppressed; and a company of them were in

[1] Syr. "in thy seed." [2] Genes. xxii. 16-18.

[3] All this is somewhat paraphrastic.

[4] Genes. xv. 2-3. [5] Syr. "thy son."

[6] Syr. "And He made him get out and said to him."

[7] Genes. xv. 4-5. The last words are somewhat paraphrastic.

[8] The *Ḳāmūs* explains this word as being a relative adjective referring to the *Jarāmiḳah* about whom see *Ṭab.* 1, 2, 827. The word seems to me to be the Syriac relative adjective "Gramḳāya" from Beit Garmai, country bordering the ancient Adiabene, on the east bank of the Tigris and the two Zabs.

[9] I.e. were called "Ishmaelites." Syriac writers even before the time of Muḥammad called the Arabs by this name. See our *Narsai Homiliae*, i. pp. 115-117; and our *Sources Syriaques*, i. pp. 111, 123, 144, and ii. p. 174.

the direction of the deserts and in the Ḥijāz, amidst hardships and wars. Those who dwelt in Egypt went, later, to Syria where war was waged against them morning and evening by those who were around them. Then they were not long in being scattered, banished, stripped of their power, deprived of their Kingdom, and dispersed in different regions and countries of the earth. Bands of black men[1] and waves of white men, molested them until the Prophet—may God bless and save him—appeared; then after a long time all the prophecies were realised and the messages fulfilled, and the children of Ishmael triumphed over those who were around them, pulverised them, scattered them in the air, as the prophets—peace be with them—had foretold, and ground them. They spread in all the regions of the earth like young locusts, and in competing with other nations they became as their life-blood,[2] and excelled them at the measure of the distance of the Pleiades from the earth, in India, Abyssinia, extreme Sūs,[3] Turkestan, and Khazar;[4] they reigned, too, in East and West, and where the waves of the Mediterranean and Euxine seas[5] collide. The name of Abraham appeared then in the mouth of all nations, morning and evening, and there is at present no man, no woman, no male slave, no female slave, rich or poor, happy or unhappy, on sea or on land, who does not believe in One God, glorify the God of Abraham, and seek His protection.

As to Judaism, it had appeared only in one section of mankind. As to Christianity, although it appeared in a great and glorious nation, yet in the land of Abraham

[1] Lit. "red." The *Tāj.* says that the two epithets "black and white" comprise all mankind, the red type being included in the word "white."

[2] Many ancient philosophers believed the soul to reside in the blood; cf. Aristotle, *De animâ* 1, 2; cf. *Levit.* xvii. 18.

[3] In Morocco.

[4] Country corresponding approximately with the ancient Hyrcania; see *Yāḳūt* (ii. 436).

[5] Lit. of the two seas: *Baḥrain.*

and his wife Sarah, and their forefathers, and in the land of Hagar and her fathers, it had not wielded the sceptre and held absolute power and sway such as those vouchsafed by God to their inhabitants through the Prophet—may God bless and save him.

In favour of what I have claimed I shall now bring testimonies from the prophets, but I should first begin by refuting that rude Garmecite who belittled Ishmael and blamed him on account of the description given him by God. Were it not for his stupidity and the weakness of his intelligence, he would have known that the words of revelation have meanings and mysteries understood only by people who are far advanced in science. The Torah said that God "became a lion and devoured the children of Israel;"[1] it is said, too, in the Torah, that "God is a burning fire;"[2] and God is neither fire nor a ravenous beast; but these are taken as illustrations for wrath, irritation, punishment, and revenge. The Christ called the head of His apostles, the one whom he ordered to shepherd his community, *Simeon the stone* (Peter); and He called all His nation *Sheep;* and He called Himself *Lamb of God.* If one were tempted to answer that stupid and weak-minded man, one would tell him that a wild ass is stronger and more powerful than a lamb which is devoured by the wolf, and coveted by the dog and the fox. There is indeed no animal among quadrupeds weaker and less powerful than it. If that ignorant dolt and his followers return to the interpretation of these names we also will begin to interpret and say:

The interpretation of the *wild ass* comprises many meanings, one of which is that God—may He be blessed and exalted—indicated by this name that Ishmael—peace be with him—would dwell in dry and arid lands, protect his consort, and be warlike and jealous, in the same way as the wild ass dwells in the deserts, castrates the male organ from his young ones out of jealousy, and attacks

[1] Num. xxiv. 9. [2] Exod. xxiv. 17.

vigorously herds pertaining to other males, not ceasing to fight against the male in kicking it and biting it, until it has conquered its female and its herd. When it has got them, it keeps them and protects them, and defends their young ones, and does not eat them as lions and wolves do; these seek victory only to devour and to gulp, but wild asses seek victory from the love of action and sport.

Further, God called Ishmael by this name in order that no means may be found for denying him—peace be with him—a dwelling in the deserts, and in order to signify that God had placed him in these deserts for a great and beautiful purpose, viz. that He, the Most High, wished to preserve his genealogy and to keep intact his freedom, in order that he might not have that slavery among the nations that others had, nor be expatriated and torn away as others have been.

Let that miserable idiot understand these meanings, and not vilify the one about whom God—may He be blessed and exalted—said that "He has blessed him and magnified him exceedingly." He who belittles him that God has magnified is like the man who magnifies him that God has belittled: suffice it to say that the one who does this does it to his shame and his confusion!

The wild ass has also the meaning which the Persians and other peoples have given to it; they called a man warlike, courageous, and skilled in the art of fighting "*Gor;*" hence Bahrām *Gor* got his surname; and *Gor* means a wild ass; through it the inhabitants of Ṭabaristān have been called *Gorīyah*, and for the same reason a bold and courageous man is called *Gor-mardān*, i.e. the wild ass of men; likewise the Arabs call a courageous man "*Ram of the tribe*," and compare him with the stallion and the male camel kept for breeding, and with other animals.

XVII.

CHAPTER X.

THE PROPHECIES OF THE PROPHETS ABOUT THE PROPHET—MAY GOD BLESS HIM AND THEM, AND SAVE HIM AND THEM.

I HAVE already mentioned four prophecies about Ishmael —peace be with him—which contain testimonies to the truth of the religion of the Prophet—may God bless and save him—which only the ignorant ignore and the stupid deny. If the Prophet—may God bless and save him—had not been sent, these prophecies would have been vain and inexplicable. I shall mention from other prophecies of the prophets—peace be with them—those which are as clear as something seen with one's own eyes. Some of them have indeed described his time, his country, his mission, his followers, his *Helpers*, and have clearly mentioned him by name.

The fifth prophecy alluding to him and pointing to his prophetic office and to his truth, is the saying of Moses—peace be with him—to the children of Israel, found in the eleventh chapter of the fifth and the last Book of the Torah: "The Lord your God will raise up from the midst of you, and from your brethren, a Prophet like unto me; unto him ye shall hearken."[1] And the Torah said, in this same chapter, in confirmation and explanation of this saying, that the Lord said to Moses—peace be with him—"I will raise them up a Prophet from among their brethren, like unto thee; and whosoever will not hearken unto my words which that man shall deliver in my name, I will avenge myself on him."[2] And God has not raised up a prophet from among the

[1] Deut. xviii. 15.

[2] Deut.. xviii. 18-19.

brethren of the children of Israel, except Muḥammad—peace be with him; the phrase "from the midst of them" acts as corroboration and limitation, viz. that he will be from the children of their father, and not from an avuncular relationship of his. As to the Christ—peace be with Him—and the rest of the prophets—may God bless them—they were from the Israelites themselves; and he who believes that the Most High God has not put a distinction between the man who is from the Jews themselves, and the man who is from their brethren, believes wrongly.

The one who might claim that this prophecy is about the Christ—peace be with Him—would overlook two peculiarities, and show ignorance in two aspects; the first is that the Christ—peace be with Him—is from the children of David, and David is from themselves, and not from their brethren; the second is that he who says once that the Christ is Creator and not created, and then pretends that the Christ is like Moses, his speech is contradictory, and his saying is inconsistent. Similarly wrong would he be who would pretend that this prophecy is about Joshua, son of Nun, because Joshua is not counted among the prophets, and has delivered nothing on behalf of God to the children of Israel, but what Moses—peace be with him—had already delivered, and also because he is from themselves, and not from their brethren.

Therefore, the prophet that the most High God "has raised up from their brethren" is Muḥammad—may God bless and save him—and whosoever contradicts him God will wreak vengeance upon him. You see already distinct traces of vengeance upon those who have rejected him, and clear marks of grace upon those who have accepted him.

And Moses said in the twentieth chapter of this Book: "The Lord came from (Mount) Sinai,[1] and rose up from Seir, and appeared from Mount Paran, with

[1] In Arabic "Sinīn," as in the Ḳur'ān xcv. 2.

tens of thousands of saints at His right hand. He gave them (power), and made them to be loved by nations, and called blessings on all His saints."[1] Paran is the land which Ishmael—peace be with him—inhabited; for this reason God had previously mentioned it in the Torah, saying "And he learned archery in the wilderness of Paran."[2] All people knew that Ishmael dwelt in Maccah, and his children and successors who are in it and around it know the abode of their grandfather, and do not ignore his land and his country;—and "the Lord" rose up from Paran! If this is not as we have mentioned, let them show us "a lord" who appeared from Mount Paran; and they will never be able to do so. The name "*lord*" refers here to the Prophet—may God bless and save him; it is a word applied by Arabs and non-Arabs to the Most High God, or to men, His servants, as if you would say "*the lord of the house*," and as the Syrians call the man whom they wish to exalt: *Mārī* = "my lord," "my master," *mār* meaning in Syriac "lord."

[1] Deut. xxxiii. 2-3. [2] Genes. xxi. 20-21.

XVIII.

THE PROPHECIES OF DAVID ABOUT THE PROPHET—MAY GOD BLESS AND SAVE BOTH OF THEM.

AND the prophet David—peace be with him—said in the forty-fifth psalm: "Therefore God hath blessed thee for ever; gird then thy sword, O giant, because thy majesty and thy *Ḥamd* are the conquering majesty and *Ḥamd*.[1] Ride thou on the word of truth and on the course[2] of piety, because thy law and thy prescriptions are associated with the majesty of thy right hand;[3] and thy arrows are sharp, and the people fall under thee."[4] We do not know anyone to whom the features of girding a sword, sharpness of arrows, majesty of the right hand, and falling down of people under him, are due, except the Prophet—may God bless and save him—who rode on the word of truth, humbled himself before God in devotion, and fought the idolaters until the true faith prevailed.

And David—peace be with him—said in the forty-eighth psalm: "Great is our Lord, and He is greatly *Maḥmūd;* and in the city of our God and in His mountain, there is a Holy One and a *Muḥammad;*[5] and the joy hath come to the whole earth."[6] This prophecy

[1] This is more in accordance with the East Syrian version which repeats twice the word "glory."

[2] Syr. "meekness."

[3] Syr. "Thy law is in the fear of thy right hand."

[4] Ps. xlv. 2-5.

[5] A not very natural rendering of a Syriac sentence meaning "In the city of our God and in His holy and glorious mountain." Strictly speaking, however, it can have the meaning given to it by the author. See below, p. 131.

[6] Ps. xlviii. 1-2.

of David—peace be with him—is clearness and explicitness itself which cannot suffer any ambiguity. David has indeed mentioned the Prophet by name.

And David—peace be with him—said in the fiftieth psalm: "God hath shown from Zion a *Maḥmūd* crown. God then shall come and shall not be idle; and fires shall devour before Him, and they shall be very tempestuous round about him."[1] Do you not see that the prophet David—peace be with him—does not strip from any of his prophecies the mention of *Muḥammad* or *Maḥmūd*, as you read it yourselves? His saying "a *maḥmūd* crown" means that he is a *Muḥammad* and a *maḥmūd* head and leader. The meaning of "Muḥammad," "Maḥmūd," and "Ḥamīd" is linguistically identical. The example of "crown" is given to mean lordship and leadership.

And he said, too, in the seventy-second psalm, in confirmation and corroboration of the preceding prophecies: "He shall have dominion from sea to sea, and from the rivers unto the end of the earth. They that dwell in the islands shall bow before him on their knees, and his enemies shall lick the dust. The kings of Tarshish and of the isles shall bring him presents, and the kings of Sheba and the kings of Seba shall offer gifts. All kings shall fall down before him, and all nations shall (obey him and) submit to him.[2] For he shall deliver (the persecuted and) the needy from him who is stronger than he, and he shall look after the weak who has no helper. He shall have mercy for the weak and the poor, and shall save their souls from harm and violence; and precious their blood shall be in his sight. And he shall remain, and to him shall be given of the gold of the countries of Sheba; and prayer shall be made for him continually, and daily shall he be blessed, like a great quantity of corn, on the surface of the earth; and he shall make his fruits grow on the top of the mountains,

[1] Ps. l. 2-3. [2] Syr. "Shall fear," or: "worship him."

like those which grow on the Lebanon; and he shall make something like the grass of the earth to shoot up in his town; and his memory shall endure for ever; his name exists before the sun, and all nations shall be blessed by him, and all of them shall give him *Ḥamd*" (or: "call him *Muḥammad*").[1]

This is an efficient and sufficient prophecy, in which there is no ambiguity and difficulty. We do not know anyone who reigned from sea to sea, and from the rivers which God has mentioned in the Torah: Tigris, Euphrates, Pison and Gihon, and before whom kings bowed on their knees, and whose enemies licked dust, and to whom the kings of Yaman brought presents, except the Prophet—may God bless and save him—and his nation, and except Maccah and the traces of Abraham's steps which it contains.[2] And we do not know anyone who is blessed and prayed for continually, except Muḥammad—may God bless and save him—in the following saying of the believing nations: "O God, pray over Muḥammad and the family of Muhammad, and bless Muhammad and the family of Muḥammad." Which sign is more obvious and which prophecy is clearer and more luminous than this, especially when the prophet David—peace be with him—closed his prophecy by saying "And all nations shall be blessed by him and call him Muḥammad?;" and the meaning of *Muḥammad* and *Maḥmūd* is one.

And David—peace be with him—said in the hundred and tenth psalm: "The Lord is at thy right hand, and He shall strike through kings in the day of His wrath; (He shall weaken the prop of the kingdom), and shall judge among them in justice.[3] He shall multiply the

[1] Ps. lxxii. 8-12, i.e. "shall praise him."

[2] Allusion to the traditional *Maḳām Ibrāhīm* containing the "stone which, yielding under the weight of Abraham, bears the impression of his foot. It is situated close to the Ka'bah.

[3] The Syriac is: "He shall judge the Gentiles."

(dead bodies) and the corpses, and shall cut off the heads of many people in the earth, and shall drink in his journey from (the water of) the valleys; therefore, His head shall be lifted up (to the heights)."[1] This is also a description as clear as something seen with the eye. Who is the one at whose right hand the Lord was, who judged in justice, who cut off heads, and who multiplied dead bodies and corpses, except him—may God bless and save him—and his nation?

And he said, too, in the hundred and forty-ninth psalm: "For the Lord hath taken pleasure in His people, and hath beautified the poor with salvation; let the saints be strong in glory, and sing to Him in their beds, and praise God with their throats; because in their hands is the two-edged sword, to execute vengeance upon the heathen, and punishment upon the nations—to bind their kings with chains, and their exalted ones (and nobles) with fetters, to bring them to the written (and decided) judgment. *Hamd* to all His saints."[2] Do you not see—may God guide you—that these peculiarities refer exclusively to the Prophet—may God bless and save him—and to his nation? It is he who has the two-edged sword with him, it is he who with his nation has executed vengeance upon the giants of Persia and the tyrants of the Greeks and others, and it is he whose followers have bound the kings with chains, and conducted their nobles and their children in chains and fetters, and who sing to God in their beds, and glorify Him morning and evening, and continually, in saying: "God is supremely great and much praise be to God."

And he—peace be with him—said in the hundred and fifty-second psalm—which is a psalm attributed to Isaiah—peace be with him—mentioning the Arabs and their country, and not leaving any room for reply and excuse "Let the wilderness and the cities thereof rejoice, and

[1] Ps. cx. 5-7. [2] Ps. cxlix. 4-9.

let (the land of) Kedar become meadows. Let the inhabitants of caves sing, and shout forth from the tops of the mountains the *Ḥamd* of the Lord, and declare His praises in the islands. For the Lord shall come forth as a mighty man, and as a man of war, stirring up for pride. He shall rebuke, shall be mighty, and shall kill His enemies."[1] To whom does the wilderness belong, O my cousins—may God guide you—except to this nation? And who is Kedar, except the descendants of Ishmael—peace be with him—who inhabit caves, and give *Ḥamd* to the Lord and declare His praises at daybreak and at midday? And who is he who rebuked, became mighty, and killed his enemies, except Muḥammad—may God bless and save him—and his nation? As to the meaning of David's saying "The Lord shall come forth," we have demonstrated above that the name "Lord" refers to men of high standing and noble.

[1] Isa. xlii. 11-13. These verses with Exod. xv. 1-21 and Deut. xxxii. 1-43 are incorporated with the psalter in the East Syrian or Nestorian breviary (*Ḅreviarium Chaldaicum*, Paris, 1886, vols. i., ii., iii., pp. 332-337).

XIX.

THE PROPHECIES OF ISAIAH ABOUT THE PROPHET—MAY GOD BLESS AND SAVE HIM.

HE said in the second chapter of his book: "The Lord will be mighty in that day and lifted up alone over all the pine-trees of Lebanon that are high and elevated, and over all the oak-trees which are in the land of Bashan, and over all the high mountains, and over every hill that is lifted up, and over every lofty tower, and over every inaccessible mountain, and over all the ships of Tarshish, and over all pleasant and handsome imagery. He will destroy the idols in an open destruction, and (people) will hide in the caves of the rocks and in the holes of the earth, from the terror of God the Most High, and from the glory of His *Ḥamd.*"[1] Isaiah is in accordance with the prophet David—peace be with both of them—who said: "Thy majesty and Thy *Ḥamd* are the conquering *Ḥamd.*"[2] It is as if these two prophecies were two rays coming from a single reflecting centre. As to the mountains and trees, they mean men of high and low estate, and kings; instances for this are numerous in their Books.

In the third chapter, he said on behalf of the Most High God: "I will lift up an ensign to the nations from a remote country, and hiss unto them from the ends of the earth, and they will come swiftly and quickly; they will not be weary, nor will they stumble; they will not slumber, neither will they sleep; they will not loose the girdle of their loins, and the latchet of their shoes will not be broken. Their arrows are sharp, and their bows

[1] Isa. ii. 12-19. [2] Cf. supra, p. 88.

are bent; and their horses' hoofs are like flint in solidity, and their wheels are as swift as whirlwinds; and their roaring is like that of lions, and like that of a young lion roaring for a prey, and no one can escape him. In that day he will overtake them like the roaring and the colliding waves of the sea; and they will look unto the earth, and they will only see distress and darkness; and the light shall be darkened from the dust of their masses."[1]

This is the saying of the Most High God. And the children of Ishmael—peace be with him—the nation of the Prophet—may God bless and save him—are those for whom God hissed; and they came from their country with haste, without weariness and sloth; their arrows were sharp, and their bows bent; the hoofs of their horses were like rock and flint, and their roaring was like the roaring of lions; it is they that had prey from East and West, and no one could escape them. The giants became like lambs with them, and dust was stirred by their onslaught, while paths and defiles were too narrow for them.

And he—peace be with him—said in the fifth chapter, in explanation of his preceding prophecies: "The nation which was in darkness saw a resplendent light, and those that were in deep darkness and under the shadow of death, light hath shined upon them. Thou hast multiplied partisans and followers of whom thou wast proud. As to them, they joy in thy hands, like those who joy in the day of harvest, and like those who joy at the division of spoils. Because thou hast broken the yoke which had humbled them, and the staff which was on their shoulders; and thou hast bruised the rod which had enslaved them, as thou hadst broken those whom thou didst break in the day of Midian."[2]

This resembles the description which the Most High God gave in the Ḳur'ān about the Prophet—may God

[1] Isa. v. 26-30. [2] Isa. ix. 2-4.

bless and save him—saying: "And he will ease them of their burden and of the yokes which were upon them."[1] See—may God guide you—and examine who is he who has broken the yoke from the children of Ishmael, destroyed the power of the enemies, and bruised the rod of the mighty. Has that light shone on anyone except on the dwellers in that dark desert of the pagan posterity of Ishmael?

And he said in this chapter: "Unto us a child is born, and unto us a son is given, whose government is on his shoulder."[2] He means by that "his prophecy is on his shoulder." All this is according to the books of the Syrians which Marcus has translated; but in Hebrew it is said "The sign of prophecy is on his shoulder."[3] This is what the Muslims call "the seal of prophecy." This is, therefore, a clear allusion to the portraiture of the Prophet—may God bless and save him—and a reference to his face and his moles."[4]

And he said in the tenth chapter, enlightening what was obscure and explaining what was difficult in his prophecies: "Thou wilt come from the country of the South,[5] from a remote country, and from the land of the desert, hastening and passing through like tempests and storms from the winds. We have seen a grievous and dreadful vision; the treacherous dealer dealeth treacherously, and the spoiler spoileth. Go up, O mountains of Elam, and mountains of Media.[6] All the object of your desire and of your dispute hath ceased. Therefore is my

[1] Kur. vii. 156. [2] Isa. ix. 6.

[3] The Hebrew also has "government" משׂרה.

[4] Cf. Ibn Taimīyah's *al-Jawāb uṣ-Ṣaḥīḥ* ii. 211. The seal of prophecy is well described by I.S. i., ii. 131.

[5] The author is playing here on the Arabic word *tayammana*, meaning to go to *Yaman*, or in the direction of the right hand, i.e. for the Northern Arabs: *Yamanwards* or *southwards*.

[6] In the text *Māhīn* (about which see *Ṭab.* i. 2627, 2632, etc.); this bears out the generally accepted opinion that "*Māh*" is to be identified with "*Mede.*" See also p. 137.

loin filled with pain, and I feel the pangs of a woman in travail. I am pained, so that I cannot hear, and I am dismayed, so that I cannot see. My heart fainteth, and dim-sightedness hath affrighted me. What I loved as agreeable and pleasant has become terrifying and as something dreadful. Prepare ye then the tables; and ye who watch and spy lift up your eyes, and eat and drink. Let the princes and the leaders rise up to their shields. Let them anoint them with ointment, for thus hath the Lord said unto me: 'Go, and set the watchman on the watch, to declare what he seeth.' And what he hath seen was a pair of horsemen, one riding on an ass, and another riding on a camel; and he hath heard great and long speech. And the watchman told me secretly and said in my ear: 'I am the permanent Lord, and I stand continually upon the watch tower and the high place of vision, day and night.' While I was in that condition, behold, one of the horsemen approached, saying: 'Babylon is fallen, is fallen, and all the graven images of her gods are broken unto the ground. That which I have heard from the mighty Lord, God of Israel, have I declared unto you.'"[1]

This, too, is a clear and obvious prophecy which only the man who deceives himself and throws away his intelligence can reject. As no reasonable man dares feign ignorance and say that there was in the world a rider on an ass more appropriate to this prophecy than the Christ—peace be with Him—so also no man with sound judgment and intelligence is allowed to say that there was in the world a rider on a camel more appropriate to this prophecy than the Prophet—may God bless and save him—and his nation.[2] Are not the men of intelligence and science amongst the *People of the Book* ashamed to attribute such a clear and sublime prophecy to some rude and barbarous people?

[1] Isa. xxi. 1-10.

[2] Cf. Ibn. Taimīyah's *Jawāb* (ibid.).

The prophet Isaiah has explained his saying, and has not left them in blindness, and has opened their deaf ears, in adding: "Thus saith the Lord, thou wilt come from the country of the South (=of Yaman)." Then he explained that by saying: "From a remote country, and from the land of the desert," in order that no objection may be left to the adversary. Then he added, saying "The gods of Babylon are fallen, are fallen, and have been destroyed." Now, there were incessantly in the country of Babylon kings who worshipped now idols, now fires, till the appearance of the Prophet—may God bless and save him—who destroyed their might, pulled down the temples of their idols and their fires, and brought them into his religion either of their free will or by force. Did not the adversaries feel abashed in saying that the rightly guided prophets, of the family of Isaac —peace be with them—prophesied about the kings of Babylon, Media, Persia, and Khuzistān,[1] and neglected to mention such an eminent Prophet and such a great and Abrahamic nation, and such a victorious Empire, or that God had hidden and concealed such a nation from them?

As to his saying "I saw a treacherous dealer dealing treacherously," he designates by it Persia, Khuzistān, and the land of Nabatia, which he has mentioned in saying to them "Go back unsuccessful to your countries, and retire like banished and plundered people."[2]

And he said in this chapter: "In the forest which is on the way to Duranim[3] shall ye lodge in the evening. O inhabitants of the South, welcome with water him that is thirsty, and receive with food the scattered and dispersed people; because the sword hath scattered them; and their dispersion was from sharp spear-heads, bent

[1] Country extending between Ahwāz, Baṣrah, and Ispahān (*Yāḳūt*, i. 497).

[2] See below about Isa. xxiv. 16-18. The sentence is misplaced.

[3] According to the Peshiṭta reading.

bows, and a grievous and fierce war."[1] Who are these thirsty people who came forth from the direction of the South, whom the Most High God has ordered the inhabitants of the country to meet? Or who are the peoples expatriated and scattered by war? And who are those whom God hath commanded to receive with water and food, except the Arabs, when they rose to fight against the neighbouring nations, Persians, Greeks, and others, who separated them from water and pasture?

And he said in the eleventh chapter: "From the ends of the earth have we heard song and hymn to the righteous and the pious, saying: 'A secret to me, a secret to me,'[2] and saying 'Woe is me; the treacherous dealers have dealt treacherously; yea the treacherous dealers have dealt treacherously. I am surrounding you, o inhabitants of the earth, with fear, pit, and snare; and he who fleeth from war shall fall into the pit; and he who cometh up out of the pit shall be taken in the snare, for the doors of heaven are open, and the foundations of the earth shake and tremble."[3] This is according to the translation of Marcus, while the Hebrew, which is the original, says "We have heard, from the ends of the earth, the voice of *Muḥammad.*"[4] And Maccah is in the ends of the earth, and on the sea-shore. Let them tell us when and in what generation have the polytheists and the unbelievers suffered such terrors, punishments, and calamities such as those they have endured under this Arab Empire?

[1] Isa. xxi. 13-14. Evidently the author did not consult the Hebrew text where there is very probably a clear mention of Arabia, which is missing in Syriac.

[2] Possibly a literal translation of the Syriac expression *Rāz lī*, meaning figuratively "woe is me."

[3] Isa. xxiv. 16-18.

[4] There is no such a thing in the Hebrew Massoretic text. The only difference between the Syriac and the Hebrew texts is that the former has "*the force of the righteous*," while the latter exhibits "*glory to the righteous.*"

And he said in the sixteenth chapter, explaining the preceding prophecies, and rebuking men of obstinacy and delusion: "Let the inhabitants of the arid desert rejoice, and let the wilderness and the desert be glad; let them blossom like the autumn crocus, and let them rejoice and flourish like a mountain goat, because they will be given by *Aḥmad* the glory of Lebanon,[1] and something like the excellency of watery meadows and luxuriant gardens. And they shall see the glory of Allah—may He be exalted and glorified—and the excellency of our God."[2] Do you not see—may God guide you—in this prophecy that Isaiah — peace be with him — has given to you and which the Revelation has mentioned the Arabian deserts and wildernesses, and the freshness, brightness, and honours prepared for them by *Aḥmad*—peace be with him? Does any doubt still disturb you, after he has mentioned him by name and described the dry desert?

And he said in the nineteenth chapter, adding more light and clearness: "Someone cried in the wilderness 'Prepare the way for the Lord, and make straight in the desert the way for our God. All the valleys shall be filled with water, and they will overflow; and the mountains and the hills shall become low; and the hillocks shall be levelled, and the rough ground shall be plain and smooth; and the glory of the Lord shall be revealed, and everyone shall see it, because the Lord hath said it.'"[3] Do you know—may God guide you—a nation which God has called from the desert and the wilderness, and to which He has made the rough places straight, the sterile lands fertile, and the dry land rich with pasture; to which He has made the valleys overflow with water, for their thirsty ones; and to which He has subjugated the giants and the kings whom He has

[1] The Syriac is simply "And in glory it (i.e. the desert) will be given the honour of Lebanon."

[2] Isa. xxxv. 1-2.

[3] Isa. xl. 3-5.

represented by the above hills and mountains—except this Arab nation for which the Tigris became like a beaten track? When they reached it, they said unanimously: "He who has protected us on land will also protect us on sea;" then they crossed it, while on the other side were Chosrau and his warriors and *Marzubans*;[1] they despised him, and they did not recoil from him when they were half naked, barefooted, and protecting their heads with nothing but their wrists.

And he said in this chapter: "The Lord God will appear with might, and His arm with strength and power. His reward is with Him, and His work before Him, like the shepherd who shepherds his flock; and He will gather His sheep with His arm, and carry them in His bosom, and He will feed Himself those that give suck."[2] We have already proved in what has preceded, and in our book of *Reply to the Different Denominations of Christians* that the words "God" and "Lord" are applied also to men. This prophecy corroborates this statement, since Isaiah declared that the "Lord God" was a man whose reward was with him, and his work before him. He alluded by this to the Prophet—may God bless and save him—because it is he whose reward was before him, and it is he who freely distributed his presents and gifts to the fighters for God's sake, from the spoils of the successes and victories which accompanied him. His saying "He is like the shepherd who shepherds his flock," is a figure of the tenderness of the Prophet—may God bless and save him—and his gentleness towards his co-religionists; because the Most High God says about him—may God bless and save him—"Now hath an Apostle come unto you from among yourselves; your iniquities press heavily upon him. He is careful over you, and towards the faithful, com-

[1] High dignitaries. The above saying is (curiously enough) reported by Michael the Syrian (ii. 423 edit. Chabot).

[2] Isa. xl. 10-11.

passionate, merciful."[1] And the Most High God said to Moses—peace be with him—"I shall make thee a god to Pharaoh."[2] And it is said in the Torah: "The sons of the Most High God saw the daughters of men that they were fair and handsome, and they took them as wives."[3] And the prophet David—may God bless and save him—said: "The Lord said to my Lord."[4] In all these passages it has been demonstrated that the two words "God" and "Lord" were applied to men.

And Isaiah—peace be with him—said in this chapter: "Who hath raised the Pious One[5] from the East, and hath called him to his foot, in order to give him the nations, and to awe by him the kings, and to make his swords as abundant as dust and earth, and his bows as numerous as disseminated sheaves? He shall overcome them and strike them in the face; then he shall bring forth peace; and shall not set off for a journey on foot."[6] This is similar to what the Most High God has said in the Ḳur'ān. About his saying "Who hath raised the Pious One from the East," the land of Ḥijāz, and that of 'Irāḳ, with their neighbourhood, are to the inhabitants of Syria, east; and Syria, to the inhabitants of Barḳah and of Ifriḳīyah is east; and the land of Yaman and that of Ḥijāz are called by the learned men, south. The one "called to the foot" of the "friend of God"[7] is the Prophet—may God bless and save him—and it is to him that God has given the nations; and it is by him that He has scolded the kings, and they were awed; and it is he whose archers and sword-bearers are innumerable; and it is by him that God has struck the nations in the face,

[1] Ḳur. ix. 129. The author's book mentioned above seems to be identical with the one mentioned below (p. 107) under the title: *Book of Reply to Christians*.

[2] Exod. vii. 1.

[3] Genes. vi. 2.

[4] Ps. cx. 1.

[5] The Syriac version has "piety."

[6] Isa. xli. 2-4.

[7] i.e. Abraham. The author alludes here also to the *Maḳām Ibrāhīm* found in the Ka'bah of Maccah. (See above, p. 90.)

has defeated and humbled them, and then has brought to them faith, which is Islām, and peace, as the Most High God says through the prophet Isaiah—peace be with him.

And he said in the twentieth chapter: "O family of Abraham, my friend, whom I have strengthened! I have called thee from the ends of the earth, and from its plateaus and elevated places; I have called thee and said to thee: Thou art my servant, and I have chosen thee; and I have not made a secret of it. Fear thou not, for I am with thee, and be not dismayed, for behold I am thy God. I have strengthened thee, then I have helped thee, and with my strong and righteous hand I have upheld thee; for that, they that have the advantage over thee shall be ashamed and confounded; and they that fight and oppose thee shall be as nothing and shall disappear, and the people who resist thee shall perish. Thou shalt seek them, and shalt not find any trace of them, because they shall cease and they shall be as something forgotten before thee; for I, the Lord, have strengthened thy right hand. I said unto thee, Fear not, because I am thy help; and thy redeemer is the Holy One of Israel, saith God the Lord. I have made thee a sharp threshing instrument which thresheth all that is under it, and beateth it thoroughly. Thou shalt do likewise; thou shalt make the mountains low and thresh them, and thou shalt make the towns and the hills as chaff that winds shall carry away and whirlwinds shall scatter; and thou shalt rejoice then and rest in the Lord, and become *Muḥammad*[1] in the Holy One of Israel."[2]

This is a living prophecy, a saying clear and not difficult, distinctly and not ambiguously worded. The man spoken to is from the family of Abraham and from the descendants of Ishmael, who are represented by a pestle which triturates and a threshing instrument which pounds the mountains in the name of the God of Muḥam-

[1] Syr. "Thou shalt be glorified." [2] Isa. xli. 8-16.

mad whom He has mentioned by name, in saying "He shall become *Muḥammad* in the Most High God." Truth has become manifest, and the veil has been withdrawn. And if a sophist squabbles here, the most he could say would be that the meaning of the Syriac word is "he became *Maḥmūd*," and not "*Muḥammad*;" but he who knows the Arabic language and is versed in its grammar will not contradict us in saying that the meaning of *Maḥmūd* and of *Muḥammad* is identical.

And he said in this chapter: "The poor and the weak seek water, and there is no water for them; their tongues have withered with thirst; and I, the Lord, will then answer their call, and will not forsake them; but I will open for them rivers on the mountains, and will make fountains flow in the desert; I will create pools of water in the wilderness, and will make springs of water flow in the dry land; I will grow, in the waste deserts, the pine-tree, the myrtle, and the olive-tree; and I will plant in the arid desert the handsome cypress, that they may all of them see, and know, and consider, and understand that the hand of God hath done this, and the Holy One of Israel hath created it."[1] O my cousins, how can you find an escape from this clear and living prophecy? What could you say about it after Isaiah mentioned the countries, described the dry lands, the deserts, and the wilderness of Arabia, the springs to which God has given outlet, the rivers which He has caused to flow, and the different kinds of trees which He has planted therein? Then Isaiah mentioned the poor and the thirsty people of the desert and of Hijāz,[2] and declared that it is the hand of the Most High God that has done it. He who rejects and throws away this prophecy has neither religion, nor shame, nor fairness. The name of the Prophet—may

[1] Isa. xli. 17-20.

[2] For the linguistic meaning given by Arab writers to the word *Ḥijāz*, see Lammens's *Le berceau de l'Islam*, p. 13. It is generally used in the sense of "barrier."

God bless and save him—having been mentioned in the preceding prophecy, what have you now left, O ye who doubt? And what would be the reasonable and acceptable excuse for the man who makes himself deaf and blind with regard to it?

And he said in the twenty-first chapter: "Let the beasts of the desert, from jackals to ostriches, honour Me and exalt Me, because I have given water in the wilderness, and I have made rivers to flow in the country of Ashimun, in order that My chosen people might drink from them; let then My people that I have chosen drink from them."[1] He who has doubts about the preceding prophecies will have no excuse in ignoring, or feigning to ignore, that the ostriches live only in the wilderness. He has mentioned the foxes and the ostriches as an illustration referring to people dwelling in the desert and the wilderness. He who squabbles about this and tries to make it ambiguous is on the way to perdition.

And he said in the twenty-second chapter, on behalf of the Most High God: "I am the Lord, and there is no God besides Me; I am He from whom no secret is hidden; I declare to (My) servants what hath not been done, before it is done, and I reveal unto them the events and the unknown things, and I will do all My pleasure: calling a bird from the desert and from the far and remote country."[2] This is the Prophet—may God bless and save him—and it is he with whom God was pleased on account of the diligence which he had shown in pleasing and loving Him. If the adversaries shout and quibble, let them tell us where are the deserts and the waste lands which the Most High God has described, and who is the man whom He has called, and who pleased Him.

And he said in the twenty-third chapter, speaking to mankind of the Prophet—may God bless and save him—"Listen, O isles, and understand, ye nations. The Lord

[1] Isa. xliii. 20-21.

[2] Isa. xlvi. 9-11.

hath invested me with majesty from far, and from the womb hath He made mention of my name. And He hath made my tongue as a sharp sword, when I was still in the womb. And He hath hidden me in the shadow of His right hand. And He hath put me in His quiver as a chosen shaft; and He hath kept me close for His secret, and said unto me 'Thou art My servant.' My piety and my justice are, therefore, before the Lord, truly; and my works are in the hands of my God,[1] and I became *Muḥammad*[2] with the Lord, and in my God are my strength and my power."[3] If somebody denies the name of *Muḥammad* in these verses, let it be then *Maḥmūd;* he will not find a way to any other objection. It is, indeed, he whose tongue has been made by God as a sword, and this tongue is the perspicuous Arabic, which He had hidden in His quiver for His secret and His divine Economy which He has revealed; and it is he who, morning and evening, says through his community "There is no strength and there is no power except by God."

And he said in the twenty-sixth chapter what would enlighten, corroborate, and confirm his preceding prophecies, and spoke to Hagar—peace be with her—"Sing, O woman of few children and desolate, and rejoice in *Ḥamd*, O barren; because the children of the deserted and the ill-treated have become more numerous than those of the fortunate and the favourite. And the Lord said to her, Enlarge the places of thy tents, and stretch forth the curtains of thy habitations. Spare not, and be not weak, but lengthen thy cords, and strengthten thy stakes, for thou shalt spread and extend in the earth, on the right hand and on the left, and thy seed shall inherit the nations, and they shall inhabit the desolate and ruined towns."[4]

[1] The author has omitted the words which refer to Jacob and Israel.

[2] Syr. "I was glorified."

[3] Isa. xlix. 1-5.

[4] Isa. liv. 1-4. The Syriac, "shall make the desolate and ruined towns inhabited." The Arabic sentence may also bear this meaning.

Would that I knew what they might say about this prophecy in which the Most High God has mentioned both Sarah and Hagar—peace be with them—and in which Isaiah—peace be with him—has described the tents of the descendants of Hagar. To whom do these refer and are suitable, but to the children of Hagar and her posterity? To whom do the tents and the tent-cords belong, except to her descendants? You would perhaps say that the prophet meant by them the Abyssinians and the Turks, because they also have tents and stakes (!) He who makes himself so blind as to reject this prophecy is really blind, having little sight for himself, and rebelling openly against his Lord; so much so that the Most High God has not left them any doubt, but has repeated, enlightened, and explained His saying.

And, on behalf of the Most High God, he said in the twenty-eighth chapter: "By Myself have I sworn, and from My mouth the word of righteousness have I shown forth, which has no contradiction and change: unto Me every knee shall bow, and by Me every tongue shall swear, and they shall say one and all that the grace is from the Lord."[1] Which is the community which swears by the name of God, and who are those who kneel down to the name of the One God, praise His grace, morning and evening, and exalt Him and pray to Him as One, except the Muslims? As to the Christians, they attribute grace and merits to the Christ, and say at the beginning of their prayers at the altars "May the grace of Jesus Christ be fulfilled on us."[2]

And Isaiah prophesied in this chapter revealing the secrets of the preceding prophecy, and rebuking blind

[1] Isa. xlv. 23-24. These verses precede the above quotations in the Book of Isaiah, but have been cited after them. The same phenomenon will also occur below, and this would imply that our MS. may be considered as a transcript from the first draft of the author's autograph.

[2] These words are found at the beginning of the Syro-Nestorian liturgy. See *Missale juxta ritum Ecclesiæ Syrorum Orientalium*, Mosul, 1901, p. --

and ignorant people. He did not leave the sophist any excuse nor the obstinate any outlet, for he spoke to Hagar, saying: "O thou plunged and immersed in pains, who hast not possessed happiness nor comfort, behold, I will set thy stones in beryl, and consolidate thy foundations in sapphire, and adorn thy walls with rubies, and thy gates with carbuncles, and embellish the borders of thy house with precious stones. All thy children shall recognise Me there, and shall not deny Me, and I shall make peace general to thy sons. In righteousness and justice shalt thou be embellished. Decline then from oppression and aversion, for thou art safe from them; and turn away from humility and lowliness, for they shall not come near thee; and whosoever is sent by Me shall come to thee, and shall dwell in thee; and thou shalt be a refuge and a protection for those who dwell and live in thee."[1] Examine this prophecy—may God guide you—since you are intelligent and skilled in controversy, and see for yourselves, since you are responsible people; do you know another "plunged and immersed in pains" besides Hagar, and does this address suit another one besides her and her children? What honour is greater and higher than the testimony of God, to the effect that all of them know Him and do not ignore Him, and that He has made their country a "refuge" and a "protection," that is to say an asylum and a place of safety. Maccah has indeed been built in mosaic work and with the best stones, and the diadems of kings have been brought into it. He who has his two ears let him hear my speech and my advice; let him ponder over these testimonies and analogies, let him sit alone with this book and with my other book entitled *Book of Reply to Christians;* let him seek true guidance from God and work for the deliverance of his soul, before its condemnation overtakes him.

He prophesied, too, in this chapter, called and cried,

[1] Isa. liv. 11-15.

saying: "O those who thirst, come ye to the water and the watering-place, and he that hath no money, let him go and take food and drink, and have wine and milk without money and without price."[1] This prophecy of Isaiah points to the grants of God to the posterity of Hagar, the nation of the Prophet—may God bless and save him—that they will go, in the world to come, to what the Most High has promised them: "rivers of wine and rivers of milk, the taste whereof changes not, and rivers of wine delicious to those who drink."[2] Ponder over the similarity and resemblance which exists between the two prophecies.

And he said in this chapter: "I have set thee as a witness to the peoples, a leader and a commander to the nations, in order that thou mightest call the nations that thou knewest not; and the nations that knew thee not will come to thee in haste and with eagerness, because of the Lord, thy God, the Holy One of Israel, who hath made thee *Aḥmad.*[3] Seek ye then what is with the Lord, and if ye know Him, listen to Him, and when He is near to you, let the sinner forsake his sin, and the unrighteous man his way, and let him return unto me that I may have mercy on him, and let him be converted to our God whose mercy and goodness are abundant."[4] He who ponders over this prophecy and examines it carefully will not be in need of any other, because Isaiah has mentioned the Prophet—may God bless and save him—by name, and has said "God hath made thee *Aḥmad.*" If the adversary prefers to say "It is not *Muḥammad*, but *Maḥmūd*," we will agree with him, because their meaning is identical. And the nations came to him in haste and eagerness, and God made him a leader to the nations, a caller to God, as Isaiah says, and an illuminating lamp.

And he said in the twenty-eighth chapter that the

[1] Isa. lv. 1.
[2] Ḳur. xlvii. 16.
[3] Syr. "has glorified thee."
[4] Isa. lv. 4-7.

Most High "God looked, and there was no justice,[1] and it displeased Him; and He saw that nobody was vindicating the truth; therefore the Lord wondered at that, and sent His intercessor, and brought salvation unto him with His arm, and upheld him with His grace. And he put on piety as a breastplate, and laid upon his head the helmet of help and salvation; and clothed himself with garments of deliverance to take vengeance upon those who hated and opposed him. To the inhabitants of the islands he will pay recompence, so that the name of God might be feared from the western parts of the earth, and his glory revered from its eastern parts."[2] The Prophet —may God bless and save him—has put on righteousness as a breastplate, laid on his head the helmet of help and salvation, clothed himself with garments of deliverance and vengeance against the enemies of God, repaid recompense to the inhabitants of the islands, and made manifest the name of God in the Eastern and Western parts of the earth, the inhabitants of which submitted to him. Where is your escape from this, and what is your argument against these prophecies realised through him? And how can a man, who has stubbornly contradicted God and deafened himself towards His revelation and His call, flee from Him?

And he prophesied in this chapter about what only the weak minded people would reject, and the most ignorant and blind would ignore; because he again mentioned Hagar, and spoke to her and to Maccah, the country of her children, saying: "Arise, and make thy lamp shine; for thy time is come and the glory of God is rising upon thee. For the darkness hath covered the earth, and fog hath overspread the nations. The Lord shall shine upon thee, and His glory shall be seen upon thee. And the Gentiles shall come to thy light, and the kings to the brightness of thy rising. Lift up thy sight round about and contemplate; they shall all gather

[1] Or: judgment.

[2] Isa. lix. 15-18.

themselves together to thee, and they shall make pilgrimage[1] to thee. Thy sons shall come to thee from a remote country, and thy daughters shall be nursed in canopies and on couches. Thy heart shall be enlarged, because the sea shall be converted unto thee, and the armies of the Gentiles shall make pilgrimage to thee,[1] and thou shalt throng with numerous camels, and thy land is too small for the files of animals which shall gather to thee. The rams of Midian and of Ephah shall be brought to thee, and the inhabitants of Sheba shall come to thee, and shall tell the favours of God, and shall praise Him. All the flocks of Kedar shall come to thee, and the lambs of Nebaioth shall minister unto thee. They shall offer on My altar what pleases Me, and then I will renew a *Ḥamd* to the house of my *maḥmadah.*"[2]

This, too—may God guide you—is a prophecy which was realised, and a sign which was fulfilled and made true; the Gentiles have come to the light of the faith, and the treasures of the sea have been converted unto this Muslim nation; the droves of the nations have gone to Maccah, and camels of high breed and files of animals have thronged its population, and the inhabitants of Yaman and of Sheba have repaired to it. What is more forceful and to the point for the enlightenment of the opponents, is that Kedar and Nebaioth are from the children of Ishmael—peace be with him—who dwelt round Maccah and became its possessors and ministers. God has indeed renewed a *Ḥamd* to the house of His *maḥmadah: Muḥammad*—may God bless and save him! If this is not so, let them then name other than the Prophet—may God bless and save him—and other than Maccah; let them compare his portrait with this description, and model his characteristics upon those of these prophecies, in order that the veil may be rent open and truth made manifest.

And he said in this chapter: "Thus saith the Lord, the inhabitants of the isles shall wait for me, with those

[1] Syr. "will come."

[2] Isa. lx. 1-7.

that are in the ships of Tarshish, as they did before. They shall bring thy sons from a remote country, their silver and their gold with them, unto the name of the Lord thy God, the Holy One of Israel, who hath made thee *Aḥmad*[1] and honoured thee. And the sons of strangers shall build up thy rampart, and their kings shall minister unto thee; and thy gates shall be open continually at all times of night and day, and they shall not be shut; and the multitudes of the Gentiles shall enter into thee, and their kings shall be brought captive to thee; for the nation and kingdom that will not serve thee shall perish,[2] yea those nations shall be utterly wasted with sword. Honour shall come unto thee from the fine pine-tree of Lebanon, and from its fir-tree, in order that My house may be made fragrant with it, and the place of My foot glorified with the abode of My honour. The sons also of them that afflicted thee shall come unto thee, and all they that harmed thee and persecuted thee shall kiss the prints of thy feet. I will set thee for honour for ever, and for beatitude and joy in all generations. And thou shalt suck the milk of the Gentiles, shalt have a share in the spoils of kings, and taste from thy raids upon them. Then thou shalt know that I am the Lord thy Saviour; because for brass I will give thee gold, and for iron silver, and for wood brass, and for stones iron; and I will make peace to be thy leader, and righteousness and justice thy might, and the Lord shall be unto thee a light and a lamp for ever."[3]

Understand, O my cousins, this prophecy, and see who it is whose rampart has been built by strangers, who has been ministered unto by mighty ones, to whom kings have been brought bound and fettered, and who wasted and destroyed with sword every kingdom and nation which did not submit to him. Do you know for the foot of the "Friend of God,"[4] a place mentioned besides

[1] Syr. "Glorified thee."
[2] Lit. "Its veils shall be scattered."
[3] Isa. lx. 9-19.
[4] Allusion to the Ka'bah; cf. pp. 90 and 101.

Maccah to which people go in the pilgrim's garb of humility, at the door of which they worship, and to which they repair from the ends of the earth in answer to the divine call?

And he said in the twenty-fourth chapter, speaking also to the Prophet—may God bless and save him—"Thus saith the Lord, the Holy One of Israel: He whose soul was despised and dishonoured, whom the nations mocked, whom the followers of the ruler scorned, before him shall kings arise when they see him, and rulers shall bow down, because the promise of God is true. It is the Holy One of Israel who hath elected thee and chosen thee, and it is He who saith: In an acceptable time have I answered thee, and in difficulties[1] have I helped thee. I have chosen thee and established thee for a covenant to the Gentiles, and light to the nations, in order that earth may be made secure by thee. Thou shalt inherit the heritages of waste places, and thou shalt say to the prisoners: Go forth and be loose, and to them that are in prison: Show yourselves and set off, and feed your flocks in the ways, because in that time your pastures shall be found in every direction and in every path. They shall not hunger nor thirst; neither shall the *simooms* nor suns smite them, because their *Raḥmān*[2] is with them; even to the springs and the fountains of water shall he guide them. And he shall make all the mountains ways and roads to them, and with them they will dispense with paths and beaten tracks. And people shall come from a far and remote country, these from the South, these from the sea, and these from the sea of Sinim. Sing, O heaven, and be joyful, O earth, and break forth into *Ḥamd*, O mountains, for the Lord hath comforted His people, and hath pitied the afflicted of His creatures."[3]

[1] Syr. and Hebr. "in the day of salvation."

[2] Name given to God in the Ḳur'ān; it is the Aramaic adjective-substantive "raḥmān," meaning "compassionate."

[3] Isa. xlix. 7-13.

This is clearness and not ambiguity, distinctness and not confusion; it is an obvious prophecy corroborating that which precedes it. By my life, it is only the Prophet and his nation whom the prophet Isaiah—peace be with him—has mentioned as being despised and dishonoured, who inherited the waste places, released the captives from prisons and bonds, and fed their flocks in the highways, after the state of siege and the hardships in which the Arabs lived under Chosrau and Caesar; and it is only to them that the mountains became ways and roads. As to the meaning of his saying "The Holy One of Israel," since he was speaking to the children of Israel, he called God by the name given Him by the children of Israel.

And he said in this chapter, a part of which he devoted to an address to Hagar and to Maccah: "I have graven thee upon the palms of my hands, therefore thy walls are continually before me. Thy children shall make haste and come to thee; and they shall drive out from thee them that wished to harm thee and destroy thee. Lift up thine eyes above and behold: they shall come to thee, and to the last man they shall gather together to thee. As I live, saith God, swearing by His name, thou shalt surely put them on as a garment, and thou shalt be adorned with crowns as a bride. And thy deserts, thy waste places, and the land to which they banished thee and in which they pressed thee, shall be too narrow for thee, by reason of the great number of their inhabitants and of them that wish to dwell therein. And they that opposed thee and swallowed thee up shall flee from thee. The children of thy restricted fecundity will say to thee 'O desolate woman of little offspring, the countries have become too strait for us; therefore clear ye away, and remove, that we may extend in their deserts.' Then thou shalt speak to thyself and say 'Who hath begotten me all these, while I am lonely, desolate, and a woman of little offspring, and while I am deserted, grieved, and enslaved?

Who hath then brought up these to me, and who hath taken care of them for me?'"[1]

Is there anything more distinct, precise, lucid, and luminous than this? God has sworn by Himelf, and His oath is true, and His engagement unbreakable—that He will make the nations as garments to be worn by them, and as an ornament for their decoration; this is true in the case of the Arabs and their Maccah, which is adorned every year with the highest silk brocades and diadems, and to which the finest pearls and ex-votos are brought from the house of the Caliphate[2] and from all the countries of the Empire; and who is the owner of the deserts and waste places, in which he was too narrowly pressed and to which he was banished, except this nomad and *Ḥijāzic* nation? And who is the woman without protection, lonely, grieved, deserted and enslaved, to whom God spoke, except Hagar? Is there any intelligent and sensible man among the adversaries who would give good advice to his soul, and pity it?

And he said in this chapter: "Thus saith the Lord, I will lift up mine hand upon the Gentiles, and set up a standard to them; and the peoples shall bring thy sons in their hands, and they shall carry thy daughters upon their shoulders. And kings shall be thy nursing fathers, and the highest and noblest among their women thy nursing mothers; and they shall bow down to thee with their face toward the earth, and lick up the dust of thy feet; and thou shalt know then that I am the Lord, and they that wait for me shall not be ashamed."[3]

This is also a prophecy which has not been vain and without object. Nations have indeed brought to Maccah—from the extreme ends of East and West, from Sind and India, from the countries of the Berbers, and from the deserts—the posterity and the descendants of Hagar born in their country, and conducted them with pomp to their home. Their kings, too, and the noblest of their

[1] Isa. xlix. 16-21. [2] i.e. Baghdad. [3] Isa. xlix. 22-23.

women nursed the sons and the daughters of Ishmael—peace be with him—and the nations bowed down to them in Maccah, with their face toward the earth in worship, and giants licked the prints of the foot of Abraham and of the feet of the Prophet—may God bless and save them—in humility, as benediction and devotion.

And he said in this chapter: "Who is this that cometh from Edom with garments more red than ripening dates?[1] I see him glorious in his garment and his attire, and mighty on account of his horses and his armies; it is I that speak in righteousness, and save the nations. It is to us an opportune day for exemplary punishment. The hour of deliverance hath become near, and the year of my salvation hath come to hand. And I looked, and there was none to help me; and I wondered that there was none to yield to my view; therefore mine own arm brought salvation unto me, and confirmed my foot with fury; and I have trodden down the people in mine anger, and I have made their frontiers waste with my wrath and my fury, and I have buried their strength under the earth."[2] Examine this also, and be not of the number of those who doubt.

And Isaiah prophesied in this chapter in addition to the preceding prophecy, and said on behalf of God: "I have made thee a name *Muḥammad;* look then from thy habitations and dwellings, O *Muḥammad,* O Holy One, for thou art the Lord, our father and our saviour, and thy name is from everlasting."[3] This is similar to the preceding prophecy of the prophet David—peace be with him—who said: "His name exists before the sun,"[4] and to his saying in the psalter: "In His mountain there is a Holy One and a *Muḥammad.*"[5]

This mention by name is sufficient for the man not overcome by his stupidity, and the period of whose

[1] So the author seems to have understood the Syriac word *Buṣar* (Bozrah). Cf. however, *Tāj*, iii. 42.

[2] Isa. lxiii. 1-6.

[3] Isa. lxiii. 14-16.

[4] Ps. lxxii. 17, cf. supra p. 90.

[5] Ps. xlviii. 1, cf. p. 88.

aberration is not lengthened. As to the meaning of the saying of Isaiah—peace be with him—that he is a "Holy One," the word "Holy" in the Syriac language means "a just and pure man;" likewise the name of "the Lord" refers to "lords," as we have already demonstrated. He who is not convinced by this prophecy and does not submit to it will openly contradict the Lord who has mentioned the Prophet twice by name, so as not to leave the adversaries in doubt. If a sophist quibbles and says that the saying of the Most High God "O Muḥammad, O Holy One," refers to the "dwellings" which He had mentioned, the Syriac text would contradict him, because if "dwellings" were intended, it would have exhibited "Holy Ones and Muḥammads," and it would not have said "Holy One and Muḥammad."[1]

And he said in this chapter: "Go through, go through the gate, and retrace the way for the nation. Level the highway, smooth it, and remove the stones from its footpaths, and lift up a standard and a road-mark for the people. For the Lord hath made His voice heard by all that are in the ends of the earth. Say thou to the daughter of Zion 'The coming of thy Saviour is near; His reward is with Him, and His work before Him.' And they shall be called a 'Holy People, redeemed by the Lord,' and thou shalt be called 'City, whose power hath been transferred to her by God from her enemies,' and 'whom her Lord hath not forsaken.'"[2] The Arabs are the holy people that the Lord has redeemed; and the city from whose enemies power has been transferred to her, and who has been avenged, is Maccah and its inhabitants. This is constant in the figurative style of the Arabs who say "Ask the city,"[3] to mean "Ask the inhabitants of the city."

[1] Strictly speaking, the Syriac text yields to the interpretation given to it by the author, because the word meaning "dwelling" (*mediāra*) is, as he says, in singular; but the Hebrew text, by having suffix-pronouns in the second member of the *status constructus*, renders 'Ali's interpretation improbable. See below, p. 130.

[2] Isa. lxii. 10-12.

[3] Ḳur. xii. 82.

XX.

THE PROPHECY OF THE PROPHET HOSEA—PEACE BE WITH HIM—ABOUT THE PROPHET—MAY GOD BLESS AND SAVE HIM.

And Hosea said: "I am the Lord God who have shepherded thee in the wilderness, and in a waste and deserted land, in which are no inhabitants and no human beings."[1] This prophecy of Hosea resembles the preceding prophecies of Isaiah. We do not know anybody that God has shepherded in the desert and in a waste land except the Prophet—may God bless and save him.

And in corroboration of his saying, he described in this chapter the Prophet's nation as glorious and mighty, to which there was not, and there shall not be a similar one, having fire burning and kindling before her, and desolation behind her. The Arab nation is that to which there was not, and there shall not be a similar one, and the Prophet is the man that God has brought up and shepherded in the arid desert and the waste wilderness. This is a concise prophecy, but sufficient to anyone whom God has favoured with His guidance. The man whose shepherd and glorifier is God Himself, and to whom God testified that there was not, and there shall not be in the world a nation more powerful and greater than his, is to be glorified by all men, and his supremacy and merits must be acknowledged. He who fails to do so is an opponent of God and in the way of rebellion and error, since the prophet Hosea—peace be with him—testified that the nation to which there was not a similar one is this Arab nation. Therefore no man of discretion and intelligence is allowed to ascribe this prophecy to John, son of Zacharias, or to any community other than that of the Muslims.

[1] Hos. xiii. 5.

XXI.

THE PROPHECY OF THE PROPHET MICAH ABOUT THE PROPHET—MAY GOD BLESS AND SAVE BOTH OF THEM.

HE said: "In the last days the mountain of the house of the Lord shall be established in the top of the mountains, and on the highest summits. And all nations shall come unto it, and many nations shall flow unto it, saying: Come, and let us go up to the mountain of the Lord."[1]

This is clearly a description of Maccah; it is to it that many nations go for pilgrimage, repairing and flowing unto it in answer to the divine call. If somebody quibbles and says that Micah meant the temple of Jerusalem, how can he be right when God showed that the event shall take place in the last days? The temple of Jerusalem was standing in the time of this prophet, who indeed must have prophesied about something which would take place in the future, and not about something of the past.

[1] Mic. iv. 1-2.

XXII.

THE PROPHECY OF THE PROPHET HABAKKUK ABOUT THE PROPHET—MAY GOD BLESS AND SAVE HIM.

IT is similar to the prophecy of Moses—peace be with him—and even clearer and more luminous than it, because it mentions the Prophet—peace be with him—twice by name. The prophet Habakkuk—peace be with him—said: "God came from the South, and the Holy One from Mount Paran. Heaven was eclipsed by the resplendence of *Muḥammad*, and the earth was full of his *Ḥamd*. The brightness of his sight shall be as the light, and he shall encircle his country with his might. Before him goes death, and rapacious birds accompany his armies. He stood and measured the earth, then he beheld the nations and pondered over them; and the everlasting mountains were scattered, and the perpetual hills did bow. The curtains of the inhabitants of Midian did tremble; and he took possession of the everlasting ways. And God was displeased against the rivers. Thine anger is in the rivers, and the wrath of thy impetuosity is in the seas. Thou didst ride on horses, and didst go up on the chariots of salvation and help. Thou shalt be filled in thy bows to overflowing,[1] and the arrows shall be drenched at thy command, O *Muḥammad*. And the earth shall be cleft with rivers. The mountains saw thee, and they trembled, and the showers of the torrent passed away from thee. The abysses gave a sound of fear, and lifted up their hands in dread and dismay. The sun and the moon stood still in their course, and the armies marched at the light of thine arrows, and at the shining

[1] This prophetic passage is ambiguously translated.

of thy spears. Thou shalt subjugate the earth in anger, and thou shalt tread upon the nations in wrath, because thou wentest forth for the salvation of thy people, and for the deliverance of the inheritance of thy fathers."[1]

This illuminating and sublime prophecy, about which there can be no doubt and suspicion, has revealed the truth, disclosed the secret, withdrawn the veils, and discarded the uncertainties. God has mentioned twice by name the Prophet—may God bless and save him—and has declared that death shall go before him, and rapacious birds shall accompany his banners, that he shall ride on horses and bring salvation, and that, at his command, the arrows shall be drenched with blood. It is he, too, to whom the sun and the moon stood still in their course, and the armies marched at the light of his arrows, and at the shining of his spears; if it is not the man we have described, who then can he be? Are they the captive and the banished children of Israel, or the peaceful and submissive Christians? How can that be, when God has mentioned the Prophet twice by name in this prophecy, described his armies and his campaigns, and declared that he will tread upon the nations and subjugate them in anger and wrath? O my cousins, leave obstinacy and chicanery, swallow the bitterness of truth, awake from your intoxication, and have right understanding about God and His just and pious prophets—peace and prayer be with all of them.

[1] Hab. iii. 3-13.

XXIII.

THE PROPHECY OF THE PROPHET ZEPHANIAH ABOUT THE PROPHET—MAY GOD BLESS AND SAVE HIM.

HE said: "Wait, saith the Lord, for the day in which I shall rise up to witness. The time hath come to show forth my determination to gather all the nations and all the kings, to pour upon them my indignation and my fierce anger. For all the earth shall be devoured with my anger and my disapproval. There I will renew to the people the chosen language, that all of them may taste the name of the Lord, and serve Him together with one consent. And in those days they shall bring me sacrifices from beyond the rivers of Kush."[1]

Zephaniah revealed and declared on behalf of God what his colleagues had delivered. He described the nation which testifies "that there is no God but one, without a partner," and the members of which gather together for His worship and bring to Him sacrifices from the shores of the Sudan and from beyond the rivers. And the chosen language is the perspicuous Arabic, which is neither unintelligible, nor barbarous, nor sophistical. It is this language which became common to the Gentiles who spoke it and were rejuvenated by the new dispensation that it brought to them.

As to Hebrew, it was already the language of those prophets. As to Syriac, never did it cross the frontiers of the country of Syria; neither did Greek cross the country of the Greeks, nor Persian the city of Irān-

[1] Zeph. iii. 8-10.

Shahr;[1] but Arabic reached as far as the spot where dust ends, the deserts of the Turks, and the countries of Khazar and India.

[1] A big city in N.W. of the province of Khurāsān about which see Le Strange's *The Lands of the Eastern Caliphate*, p. 382 seq. That the Persian language was not spoken beyond this city is historically interesting. Yāḳūt (iv. 857), however, believes that Irān-Shahr is the name of the country between Jaihūn and Ḳādisīyah. Cf. the article "Amū-Daryā" in the *Encyclopædia of Islām*, i. p. 339 seq. In the text Irān-Shahr is pr bably to be identified with Naysābūr (see Le Strange, ibid.).

XXIV.

THE PROPHECY OF THE PROPHET ZECHARIAH ABOUT THE PROPHET—MAY GOD BLESS AND SAVE THEM—WHICH CORROBORATES THE PROPHECY OF ZEPHANIAH—PEACE BE WITH HIM.

"THE Lord God shall be in that day the king of all the earth; in that day He shall be One Lord, and His name shall be one."[1] This prophecy has been realised, and the revelation has been fulfilled, and the religion has become one, and the Lord One, without dualism and Trinity in Him, without addition of anything to Him, and negation of any of His divine attributes; and His name has become one without any ambiguity or partnership.

And Zechariah—peace be with him—said also: "In that day the holiness of the Lord shall be even upon the bridle of the horse."[2] The "holiness of the Lord" means here the name of the Lord and that of His Prophet—peace be with him; and this name is found to-day on every dress, habitation, weapon, and the like; the day which the Most High God has described is, therefore, the Prophet's day.

[1] Zech. xiv. 9.

[2] Zech. xiv. 20.

XXV.

THE PROPHECY OF THE PROPHET JEREMIAH ABOUT THE PROPHET—MAY GOD BLESS AND SAVE BOTH OF THEM.

It is similar to the prophecies of Isaiah and of other prophets—peace be with them—and God spoke in it to the Prophet—peace be with him. He said in the first chapter: "Before I formed thee in the belly I knew thee; and before thou camest forth out of the womb I sanctified thee, and I appointed thee a prophet unto the nations. For whatsoever I command thee thou shalt proclaim, and thou shalt go to all that I shall send thee. And I am with thee to deliver thee, saith the Lord. And I have poured forth my speech in thy mouth; examine and see, I have this day set thee over the nations and over the kingdoms to root out, pull down, destroy, pulverise, build, and plant, whom thou pleasest."[1]

Jeremiah—peace be with him—agrees with the prophecies of his colleagues, and corroborates, confirms, and strengthens them; he describes the man who poured forth the word of God from his mouth, and whom God has empowered to root out nations, destroy nations, pulverise nations, and preserve nations. Be satisfied with this for your knowledge, and take it as a decisive evidence. May God make Islām to be your religion, and may He count you in the number of His victorious servants! A God-fearing inquirer will never find a way to ascribe this prophecy to a Christian, a Jew, or to any other.

And he said in the fourth chapter: "I will incite against you from far, O children of Israel, a mighty nation, an ancient nation, a nation whose language is not

[1] Jer. i. 5-10.

understood, and whose men are one and all skilled in warfare and mighty."[1] The Arab nation is the mighty nation whose language was not understood by the children of Israel; each member of this nation is skilled in warfare and mighty; and it is to them that the new language, mentioned by God through the prophet Zephaniah—peace be with him—belongs.

And he said in the nineteenth chapter: "After those days, I will put my law in their mouths, and write it in their hearts, and will be their God, and they shall be my people. And a man shall not need to teach his brother and his neighbour faith and religion, nor to say to them 'Know the Lord;' for they shall all know Him, from the least of them unto the greatest of them. Because of that, I will forgive their iniquity, and will no more remind them of their sins."[2]

The promise of God has been fulfilled, because He has planted His love in the hearts of the least and the greatest men of this Muslim community, and has caused their tongues to proclaim His holy prescriptions and His praises. Each one of them knows God and believes in Him: their sons, their daughters, their slaves, and their bond-servants. You will not find an agriculturist, a seaman, a groom, a sweeper, a small child, or a grown-up man, who could not, after having made his ablutions, read something from the Ḳur'ān, recite correctly his prayer alone, and make his profession in God as one, and praise Him.[3] It is for this that God has called them His people, and was pleased to choose them for Himself. These meanings cannot be ascribed to any other besides the Muslims. And God is gracious to the worlds![4]

And he said in the thirty-first chapter: "The Lord saith: I will break the bow of Elam, the chief of their might and of their power. And against Elam will I rouse four winds from the four quarters of heaven, and will

[1] Jer. v. 15-16.
[2] Jer. xxxi. 33-34.
[3] Allusion to the Muslim formula.
[4] Ḳur. iii. 146.

scatter its inhabitants towards all those quarters, until there shall be no nation where the outcasts and the scattered ones shall not be found. For I will scatter Elam before their enemies, and discomfit them before them that seek their life; and I will bring evil and fierce anger upon them, and I will send the sword after them, till I have consumed them. And I will set my throne in Elam, and will destroy from thence kings and potentates that are there. This is the saying of the Lord."[1]

Elam is Ahwāz and its dependencies. The prophets mentioned it while they were themselves in Syria. When the Persian kings transferred their seat from Persia, they came and established their residence in Ahwāz and settled in it; then, after a long period, they moved to Sawād.[2] The prophet—peace be with him—mentioned, therefore, Elam, because its name embraced all the Empire; and indeed, Elam has never experienced general discomfiture and destruction similar to those she has endured through this Arab Empire. If somebody thinks here of Alexander and his victory, or of Tubba' and his incursion, what will make him abandon his opinion and vitiate it, and discard every doubt from him, is the saying of God—may His name be blessed—"I will set my throne in Elam," that is to say, in the country of Babylon; moreover, Alexander and the Tababi'ah were not related to the belief in God.

There is another wonderful mystery in this prophecy; it is that the Most High God has represented by it this 'Abbassid Empire, and the dwelling in the land of 'Irāḳ of the Caliphs from the family of 'Abbās, by His saying "I will set my throne in Elam." It is their appanage, which only the feeble-minded ignore. As to the Umayyads, their residence was in Damascus.

If somebody asks about the "throne," I will say that it means the power of God, and His prophecy which is

[1] Jer. xlix. 35-38.

[2] Country embracing a tract of land wider than that of 'Irāḳ, and corresponding approximately to the country of the middle and lower Mesopotamia—with a few towns of the S.W. parts of Persia (cf. *Yāḳūt*, iii. 174).

living in the lands of Elam and 'Irāḳ, and in the littorals, islands, and districts of other countries in which there are mosques and oratories where hymns and praises are sung by the inhabitants, at every instant and moment of night and day. Jeremiah made mention of Elam, because the kings were in that time related to it, in the same way as the inhabitants of this country were related to the Persians in the days of the Persians, and are in our days related to the Arabs because the Arabs conquered them. As a proof to my statement that the meaning of "throne" is "power," is the saying of the prophet David—peace be with him—"Thy throne, O God, is for ever and ever,"[1] i.e. thy power and thy might.

And he said in the thirty-second chapter, speaking to the Prophet—may God bless and save him—"Prepare ye weapons of war to Me, for with thee will I scatter the nations, and with thee will I scatter the horses and their riders, and with thee will I scatter the chariots and their riders, and with thee will I scatter the young among men and women, and with thee will I scatter the shepherd and his flock, and with thee will I scatter the husbandman and his yoke of oxen, and with thee will I scatter the tyrants and the rulers; and I will punish Babylon and all the inhabitants of the countries of the Chaldaeans for all the crimes that they have done; this is the saying of the Lord."[2]

God has made this prophecy as a sequel to the preceding one, to which it is similar, and with which it is almost identical. He has indeed inflicted on the countries of the Chaldaeans and of Babylon what He had threatened them with, and has broken up their composed state of affairs, defeated their plans, destroyed their divinities, and revenged Himself on them; and what a revenge! And has destroyed them; and what a destruction! It is said that the kings of Babylon were for a long time related to Kalwādha, which is near the "City of Peace."[3]

[1] Ps. xlv. 6. [2] Jer. li. 20-24.
[3] I.e. Baghdad. About Kalwādha see *Yāḳūt*, iv. 301.

XXVI.

THE PROPHECY OF THE PROPHET EZEKIEL ABOUT THE PROPHET—PEACE BE WITH BOTH OF THEM.

He said in the ninth chapter: "Thy mother is planted on the water in thy blood, and she is like a vine which brought forth its fruits and its branches, by reason of many waters. Branches sprang up from it like strong rods standing high up over the branches of the nobles and the rulers; their boughs became lofty and surpassed all others, and their stature was enhanced by their height and the thickness of their branches. But that vine was plucked up in fury, she was cast down to the ground, and the *simooms* dried up her fruits; her strength was scattered, and the rods of her might withered, and the fire came and consumed them. Then a plant was planted in the wilderness, in the neglected, dry and thirsty land. And fire went out of her lofty rods, which devoured the fruits (of the first plant); so that she had no strong rod nor a branch to rise up for the power of authority."[1]

He who has questioned the preceding prophecy and quibbled over it, will be silenced and convinced by this one. God—may His name be blessed—has told us that He will extirpate the root of the Jews, destroy the mass of them, and annihilate their might and their beauty, which He has compared with the vine, together with its rods and branches. Then He added an illuminating and clear saying, when He—may He be blessed and exalted—declared that He will plant a new plant in the wilderness, and in the neglected and dry land, the branches of

[1] Ezek. xix. 10-14.

which shall bring forth a fire which will devour the branches of the first vine in order that no strong rod and no branch should be found in it to rise up to power and authority. The meaning of "rod" and "branch" is power.[1] And the power of the Jews and their might have disappeared from the surface of the earth, and another strong rod, yea, many other strong rods and branches rose up to a mighty power and a firm and civilised administration. In that the above prophecy has been realised.

And Ezekiel—peace be with him—said at the end of his book that God showed him a house the plan and the bounds of which an angel was directing. He described its pillars, its halls, its court-yards, and its doors; and the angel told him to remember all these and to ponder over them. But since the description of this house was too long, I noticed that people either deliberately or carelessly have believed it to be unintelligible and ambiguous; therefore I did not mention it; but on the evidence of numerous and obvious prophecies and testimonies it is clear that the description of the house that God planned and sketched through the prophet Ezekiel—peace be with him—applies to Maccah, because it contains features which do not fit the temple of Jerusalem, built after the return from the deportation to Babylon. If somebody rejects this, let him put the description in harmony with the temple built in Jerusalem, in order that we may believe him; if he fails, let him then believe what we have told him and declared to him.

COROLLARY.

If a contentious disputant rejects what we have said and pretends that the process whereby I have extracted the name of the Prophet from the above prophecies is not right, on the ground that the sentences are not preceded in Syriac by the vocative particle, the reason being that when the Syrians use a noun in the vocative form they

[1] The Arabic word used means both "branch" and "sceptre."

prefix to it the vocative particle *yā*, as the Arabs do, the following examples shall be his answer:

It is said in the Torah that God called Adam in Paradise and said to him, "Where art thou, Adam?"[1] i.e. *O* Adam. Simon Cephas spoke to the Jews and said "Hear my words, men of Israel,"[2] i.e. *O* men of Israel. In the Book of the Acts it is said that the Christ said to Paul "Saul, Saul, why persecutest thou me?"[3] i.e. *O* Saul, *O* Saul. The angel called Hagar and said "Hagar, Sarai's maid, whence camest thou?"[4] i.e. *O* Hagar. Isaiah said "Seed of my friend Abraham whom I have strengthened,"[5] i.e. *O* seed. And Isaiah said "Sing, barren, thou that didst not bear,"[6] i.e. *O* barren. And he said, too, "Seed of evildoers, and children that are corrupters, you have forsaken the Lord and provoked the Holy One of Israel,"[7] i.e. *O* seed of evildoers and *O* children that are corrupters. All these quotations suffice to prove that the vocative is not preceded in Syriac by a *yā* as in Arabic.[8]

As to what the obstinate disputants among the Christians say about the Syriac word *Mshabbḥa* that it is not *Muḥammad*, but *Mumajjad* or *Musabbah*, we may answer that it is not said to a man "Thou art the praised one," nor "Praise be to thee," because this is said only to the Most High God, who, in many prophecies, said "O Muḥammad," as I have demonstrated.[9] The adversary

[1] Genes. iii. 9. [2] Acts ii. 22. [3] Acts ix. 4.

[4] Genes. xvi. 8. [5] Isa. xli. 8.

[6] Isa. liv. 1. [7] Isa. i. 4.

[8] The above quotations refer to the Syriac text in which the vocative is not preceded by *O!*

[9] These three Arabic adjectives although not quite synonymous have many identical meanings. The main argument of the author is that the Syriac word *mshabbḥa* cannot be translated by the Arabic *mumajjad* and *musabbaḥ*, because these are adjectives applied exclusively to God. This holds good especially in the Arabic language, but the translation of *Mshabbḥa* by *Muḥammad* is lexicographically correct, with the exception that the author has built too much on it. So, for instance, when Isaiah

who rejects this and wants to make it ambiguous, may be asked to say in Syriac "praise be to God;" he will express this sentence and translate it invariably by "*Shubḥa L'alāha;*" if *Shubḥa* is translated by *Ḥamd*, *Mshabbḥa* is, therefore, *Muḥammad.*[1] And the prophet David—peace be with him—said, "Thy throne, God, is for ever and ever," i.e. *O* God.[2]

If this adversary quibbles and is resolute in pretending that *Mshabbḥa* is *Mumajjad* and not *Muḥammad*, let him tell us who is this *Mumajjad*, of whom God said through Habakkuk that "Heaven was eclipsed by the resplendence of *Mumajjad*," and "before whom goes death," and "whose armies are accompanied by rapacious birds," and "at whose command the arrows were drenched, and the armies marched at the light of his arrows," and who "subjugated the nations," and "came forth for the salvation of his people, and for the deliverance of the inheritance of his fathers;"[3] or of whom David said "Prayer shall be made for him continually, and daily shall he be blessed,"[4] while this is the saying of the believing nations: "O God, pray over Muḥammad and the family of Muḥammad, and bless Muḥammad

says: "Look from thy holy and glorious mountain" (lxiii. 14-16), the apologist separates the adjective "glorious" from its substantive "habitation," makes a substantive of "glorious" on the ground that the Syriac does not require the vocative particle *O* before the substantive, and finds in it the name of *Muḥammad* by translating "Look from thy habitations and dwellings, O Muhammad, O Holy One." In Kastallani's *Mawāhib* and in Yaḥṣubi's *Shifā* the word "Mushaffaḥ" is one of the names of Muḥammad (see ibid. the Chapter of the Prophet's names, and cf. the following note).

[1] Cf. *Khamīs*, i. 206; and Goldziher, in *Z.D.M.G.* 32, 374.

[2] Ps. xlv. 6. The author has probably forgotten to place this sentence in the list of the above quotations, of which it constitutes an integral part, and this induces us to suppose that the present MS. is a transcript from a first draft in the author's autograph. The same phenomenon occurs in the prophecies of Isaiah and in some sayings of the Prophet and the Pious Caliphs reported above.

[3] Habak. iii. 2-12; see p. 119.

[4] Ps. lxxii. 14; see p. 89.

and the family of Muhammad." Further, let him tell us who is he of whom the prophet Isaiah said "I have established thee a witness to the nations, and a king and a ruler to the gentiles,"[1] while this is the saying of the believing nations: "I testify that there is no God but Allah, and that Muhammad is the Apostle of Allah."

And who would be the *Mumajjad*, of whom God says through Isaiah "I have made thee a name *Muḥammad;* look then from thy habitations, O Holy One, O *Muḥammad.*"[2] If Isaiah meant *Mumajjad*, who would this *Mumajjad* be, except *Muḥammad?* In this there is sufficient admonition, warning, and instruction to the man whose happiness and instruction are desired by God.

[1] Isa. xlix. 8; see p. 112. [2] Isa. lxiii. 14-16; see p. 115.

XXVII.

THE PROPHECY OF THE PROPHET DANIEL ABOUT THE PROPHET—PEACE BE WITH BOTH OF THEM.

It corroborates the preceding prophecies of Ezekiel and others, and confirms our saying that the Prophet—may God bless and save him—is the last of the prophets, that his victory is from God, that he is the owner of the solid Empire after which there is no other Empire, that there is no nation similar to his nation, and that all the prophecies of the prophets which we have quoted are about him and refer to him, to the exclusion of every other.

What we find in the prophecy of the prophet Daniel —peace be with him—in the first chapter of his Book, is that he said through the Holy Spirit to Nebuchadnezzar who had asked him anent the interpretation of a vision which he had seen, without having previously told it to him: "Thou, O King, sawest a great image whose brightness was excellent, standing before thee. His head was of pure and fine gold, his forearm of silver, his belly and his thighs of brass, his legs of iron, and his feet part of iron and part of potter's clay. And thou sawest that a stone was cut out without any cutter, which smote the image upon his feet and pounded them; then the image was broken to pieces, with his iron, his brass, his silver, and his gold, and was broken in pieces like the thin chaff in the threshing-floors; and the wind carried it away, and no trace of it was found. And the stone that smote that image became a great mountain which filled the whole earth. This is thy vision, O King. Thou art this head of gold that thou sawest, and after thee shall arise another kingdom inferior to thee. The third kingdom resembling brass shall bear rule over all the earth; and the fourth kingdom shall be strong as iron: forasmuch as iron breaketh all things in pieces, shall it break everything in pieces. As to the foot which was part of iron and part of potter's clay, the kingdom shall be partly strong, and partly weak; and the union of the kingdom shall be shattered.

"And in those days the God of heaven shall set up an everlasting and eternal kingdom, which shall not change nor perish, and which shall not leave to other nations any kingdom and power; but it shall break and destroy all the kingdoms; as to it, it shall stand for ever. This is the interpretation of the stone that thou sawest cut out of the mountain without any cutter, and that brake in pieces the iron, the brass, and the potter's clay. The great God hath made known to thee what shall come to pass at the end of the time."[1]

This is an obvious prophecy and a clear allusion which does not need further explanation than that of the Prophet Daniel—peace be with him—who has verified all the above prophecies and testified that all of them refer to Muḥammad—peace be with him—and not to another one. He has told us that the last kingdom and empire will be the kingdom that the God of heaven shall set up, which will embrace all the kingdoms of the earth, stand for ever, and not leave any other kingdom and power without breaking it into pieces and shattering it. The Prophet Muḥammad—may God bless and save him—has been called the last of the prophets, because all the prophecies did not go beyond him, as you see, and because all the previous messages have been fulfilled through him, as you find and read. After him there was no prophecy and no revelation, because God had declared that no kingdom and no power shall rise after his kingdom and after his time. What objection remains, and what error stands with this prophecy? What would be, with God, the excuse of the

[1] Dan. ii. 31-45.

man who rejects it? Will he have with Him anything but torment and fire? God has said that the "God of heaven" will set up this everlasting and eternal kingdom.

And Daniel—peace be with him—said in the fourth chapter, in confirmation and corroboration of the first prophecy: "I saw in my vision that the four winds were stirred up, and that because of them the great sea became rough and exceedingly stormy. And four great beasts came out of the sea, different in form. The first was like a lion, and had eagle's wings, and I saw that its wing was plucked; and it rose up, and stood on the earth as a man, and a man's heart was given to it. And the second beast was like to a bear, standing on one side, and having three ribs in its mouth; and I heard somebody say to it: Arise, devour flesh, and eat thy fill of it. The third beast was like to a leopard, which had on both its sides four wings like the wings of a fowl, and had also four heads; and dominion was given to it. And I saw a fourth beast, great, strong, and powerful exceedingly; and it had great iron teeth, and devoured and brake in pieces, and stamped the residue with the feet of it; and I saw that it was diverse from the other beasts; and it had ten horns, the meaning of which I was considering.[1] And behold there came up among these horns another little horn, before which three of the other horns were plucked up and fell.

"Then I wished to know the meaning of the fourth beast which was diverse from all the others, what it was and what was the meaning of its ten horns, of its iron teeth, its brass nails and claws; and what was the meaning of its devouring, breaking in pieces, and stamping the residue with its feet; and what was the meaning of the little horn which came up from it, before which three horns fell, and what was the meaning of the eyes that this horn had. And I heard this horn speaking with

[1] The author gives a wrong translation of the Syriac verb *istakkal*, which he renders literally by "I was understanding." When followed by *a baith* the verb means "to consider."

remarkable speech from its mouth; the growth of this little horn, its excrescence, and its stature were more stout than those of the others. And it made war with the holy saints, and prevailed against them. And the Lord said to me: The meaning of the fourth beast is that a fourth kingdom shall rise up upon the earth, which shall be greater and higher than all the kingdoms. It shall dominate all the earth, tread it down, break it in pieces, and devour it completely. And the meaning of the ten horns is that ten kings shall arise from that kingdom; and another king shall arise after them, greater and stronger than the first ones, who shall subdue three kings."[1]

This is a clear and distinct prophecy, which does not need more explanation and elucidation than those given to it by Daniel—peace be with him. The fourth beast, of which he said that it was great, dreadful, terrible, strong, and powerful, is the image of this Arab kingdom, about which God said that it shall be the greatest and the highest of all kingdoms, and that it shall dominate all the earth, tread it down under its feet, and devour it completely. It is also the latest kingdom; and this testifies to the fact that the Prophet—may God bless and save him—is the last prophet; that all prophecies were realised through him, ended with him, and did not go beyond him. To this all the preceding prophecies pointed and referred. Blessed is the One who predetermined this and foretold it to His servants, through His prophets, prior to its realization, and who, by means of it, brought in a verdict in our favour, and strengthened our failing vision to see clearly the weakness of the adversaries' argumentation!

These are the prophecies of the prophets from the children of Israel. I shall relate now the prophecies of the Christ—peace be with Him—and of His disciples, after Him. The former have clearly referred to the time

[1] Dan. vii. 2-8; 19-24.

of the Prophet—peace be with him—and distinctly pointed to it. Those who interpreted the Books of the Christians said that the first beast was the kingdom of Babylon, as Daniel said; the second, the kingdom of the Medians; and the third, the kingdom of the Persians. The fourth is therefore without doubt the kingdom of the Arabs, the everlasting kingdom, of which God said that it shall not perish, and shall not leave any kingdom and power to another nation. This is a corroboration of the saying of the prophet Moses—peace be with him—who, on behalf of God, said about Ishmael—peace be with him—"I have blessed him and increased him exceedingly."[1]

I have found also another resplendent and wonderful prophecy in the Books of Daniel. He says: "Blessed is he that waiteth, and cometh to the thousand three hundred and five and thirty days."[2] I have carefully examined this, and found that it refers to the Muslim faith, and more especially to this 'Abbasid kingdom; indeed Daniel must have meant by this number either days, or months, or years, or a prophetic mystery that arithmetic might discover. If somebody says that he meant days, the answer is that no joy and no gladdening event took place after four years, either to the children of Israel or to the world at large. This will also be the case after one thousand three hundred and thirty-five months, because this number gives one hundred and eleven years, and some months.

If they say that he meant years, the number would end with this 'Abbāsid kingdom, because from the time of Daniel to that of the Christ there are about five hundred years. The proof of this is what has been revealed to him that he and his people shall remain seventy weeks in the deportation, then they shall return to Jerusalem, and the Messiah shall be sent.[3] And from the

[1] Genes. xvii. 20 (cf. supra, p. 77). In the above lines the word used for *Medians* is *Māhīn*, as in p. 95.

[2] Dan. xii. 12.

[3] Cf. Dan. ix. 24-25.

time of the Messiah to this year there are eight hundred and sixty-seven years.[1] This, in counting from our time, reaches this 'Abbasid kingdom, with a difference of something more than thirty years.[2] If somebody says that the prophetic days do not mean years, but a mystery that arithmetic by alphabet might find out, I thought also of that, and discovered that the number of these days was equivalent to the total of the numerical value of the letters of the words *Muḥammad Khātimul-Anbiā Mahdī Mājid*,[3] because if the numerical value of these vocables is calculated, it will give what we have shown; and they are five words.

If somebody says that it is possible that this number might also be obtained for other persons by the same arithmetical method as that whereby I found it out for the Prophet, that which would testify to the veracity of

[1] The present Defence was certainly written under the reign of Mutawakkil whose murder is fixed on the 10th of Dec., 861. This apparent anachronism may possibly be explained by the chronology adopted by the majority of the ancient Syrian writers in connection with the life of the Prophet whom they believed to have been born in the year 892 of the Seleucids, instead of 882 (Barhebræus, *Chron. Arab.* p. 160; edit. Beirut). This would give the Christian date 857 (A.H. 243). Further, it is a well-known fact that between the Seleucid era adopted in the Syrian Churches and that followed in the West there are two years of difference, these having been added by some Western writers to the Eastern computation. If we take these two years into account we should ascribe the composition of the present work to A.D. 855 (A.H. 241), or the 9th year of Mutawakkil's caliphate. On the other hand, the year of the Hijrah 622 is rightly calculated by almost all the Syrian historians and fixed at 933 of the Seleucids = A.D. 622. See Michael the Syrian, ii. 403 (edit. Chabot). As the years of the Seleucids and not those of the Christian era were used in the Eastern Churches till about the 16th century, it is even possible to suppose that the historians of the Court had miscalculated the time that had elapsed between the birth of Christ and the Hijrah.

[2] Prophecy of Daniel: 1335; Daniel's time to that of the author according to his own computation: 1367; the difference: 32. For other attempts to apply this number to Muḥammad, see Bīrūnī's *Chronology* (edit. Sachau), p. 22.

[3] I.e. "Muḥammad, the last prophet, the Mahdi, the illustrious."

what I have said, and ascribe this mystery exclusively to the Prophet—may God bless and save him—is the testimony of Daniel and of other prophets for him in the way I have already demonstrated. We will agree with the one who would apply it to another name, if this name carries with it testimonies from the prophets like those included in the name of the Prophet—peace be with him— ; but he will never be able to find such a name. Indeed, some Christians have attributed this number to the Christ, through the same method of computation, but I have contradicted them, and by testimonies from the prophets, have shown clearly that its attribution to the Prophet—peace be with him—is more appropriate than to Christ.

XXVIII.

THE PROPHECY OF THE CHRIST ABOUT THE PROPHET—MAY GOD BLESS AND SAVE BOTH OF THEM.

On this subject the Christ—peace be with Him—uttered a sentence recorded and perpetuated in the Book of the Apostle John, in the fifteenth chapter of his Gospel: "The Paraclet, the Spirit of truth, whom my father will send in my name, He shall teach you everything."[1] The Paraclet, then, whom God would send after the Christ, and who would testify to the name of the Christ—peace be with Him—is the One who would teach mankind everything that they did not know before; now among the disciples of the Christ there has not been, down to our time, a single one who taught mankind anything besides what the Christ had already taught; the Paraclet, therefore, who taught mankind what they did not know before, is the Prophet—may God bless and save him—and the Ḳur'ân is the knowledge that the Christ has called "everything."

And John said about Him in the sixteenth chapter: "If I go not away, the Paraclet will not come unto you. And when He is come, He will reprove the world of sin. He shall not speak anything of himself, but will direct you in all truth, and will announce to you events and hidden things."[2] John said, too, about Him: "I will pray my Father to give you another Paraclet who will be with you for ever."[3]

The interpretation of the saying "He will send in my name," is this: as the Christ was called Paraclet, and

[1] Joh. xiv. 26 (Syr. "The Holy Spirit").
[2] Joh. xvi. 7, 8, 13. [3] Joh. xiv. 16.

Muḥammad also was called by the same name,[1] it was not strange on the part of Christ to have said "He will send in my name," that is to say He will be "my namesake" (or: "my equal," *sami*). Indeed, it seldom happens that the Christ—peace be with Him—is mentioned in a chapter of the Books of the prophets—peace be with them—without a simultaneous mention of the Prophet—may God bless and save him—as adhering to Him and making one pair with Him, because he came after Him.

When I examined carefully the word "Paraclet," and searched deeply for the meaning of the saying of the Christ, I found another wonderful mystery in it; it is that if somebody counts the total of the numerical value of its letters, it will be equivalent to the same total as that of the letters of the words: *Muḥammad bin 'Abdallāh, an-Nabbīyul-Hādi.*[2] If somebody says that one number is missing, because the word is *Paracleta*,[3] we will answer that the letter *Alif* is a paragogical addition to the Syriac nouns. The words which would exactly be equivalent to the numerical value of the word, without any addition and diminution, are *Muḥammad Rasūlun Ḥabibun Ṭayyibun.*[4] If someone says that the same number is obtainable from other names, this will not be possible for him until he brings forth, from a scriptural evidence, the man who would answer to the description given by the Christ in His saying: "The Paraclet whom He will send, the Spirit of truth whom my Father will send in my name, He shall teach you everything;" and he will not be able to find a way for that.

And the disciple John said in his Epistle found in the Book of the Acts which is the history of the Apostles:[5]

[1] In the *Shifā* of Yaḥṣubi "Paraclet" is given as a name of Muḥammad. (In the chapter of the Prophet's names.)

[2] I.e. "Muḥammad, the rightly guiding Prophet, son of 'Abdallah."

[3] According to the Syriac pronunciation.

[4] I.e. "Muḥammad is a beloved and good apostle."

[5] The Bible used by the author incorporated the Acts and the Catholic Epistles under one title *Praxis*, as it is in the Syrian Churches.

"My beloved, believe not every spirit, but discern the spirits that are of God. Every spirit that confesseth that Jesus Christ hath come and was in flesh is of God, and every spirit that confesseth not that the Christ was in flesh, is not of God."[1] The Prophet—may God bless and save him—has believed that the Christ has come, that He was in flesh, and that He was the "Spirit of God and His word which He cast into Mary."[2] His spirit, therefore, is, on the testimony of John and of others, a true and just spirit, coming from the Most High God, and the spirit of those who pretend that the Christ is neither in flesh nor a man is from somebody outside God.

And Simon Cephas, the head of the Apostles, said in the Book of the Acts: "The time hath come that judgment must begin at the house of God."[3] The interpretation of this is that the meaning of the house of God mentioned by the Apostle is Maccah, and it is there and not at another place that the new judgment began. If somebody says that he meant the judgment of the Jews, the answer is that the Christ had already told them that "There shall not be left in the temple one stone upon another that shall not be thrown down, and remain in destruction till the day of the Resurrection."[4]

It has become evident that the new judgment mentioned by the Apostle is the religion of Islām and its judgment. This is similar to the saying of the prophet Zephaniah—peace be with him—who said on behalf of God: "I will renew to the people a chosen language;"[5] Arabic was the new and the chosen language for the new judgment and religion. Daniel, too—peace be with him—said in this sense what we have already mentioned. There was not in that time a house related to God to which the adversary might cling and say that the judgment began there, except Maccah. If somebody says that

[1] I Joh. iv. 1-3.
[2] Ḳur. iv. 169.
[3] I Pet. iv. 17.
[4] Matth. xxiv. 2, etc.
[5] Zeph. iii. 9 (cf. supra, p. 121).

the Apostle meant the Christian religion, how could he say about a religion and a judgment which had already appeared for some time: "The time hath come that it must begin"? This is an impossible hypothesis.

And the evangelist Luke reports in the eleventh chapter of his Gospel that the Christ said to His disciples: "When I sent you without purse, and scrip, and shoes, were ye harmed and lacked ye in anything? And they said: No. Then He said: But now he that hath no purse let him buy one, and likewise a scrip; and he that hath no sword, let him sell his garment, and buy a sword with it for himself."[1] The laws and prescriptions that the Christ had promulgated and preached were only submission, resignation, and obedience; when, then, at the end of His life He ordered His disciples and the standard-bearers of His religion to sell their garments in order to buy swords, men of discernment and intelligence know that He referred to another Dispensation, viz. to that of the Prophet—may God bless and save him—in pointing to his swords and his arrows which the prophets had described prior to His coming.

Simon Cephas unsheathed his sword and drew it out of its scabbard, in the night in which the Jews seized the Christ, and struck with it one of the soldiers, and cut off his ear; but the Christ—peace be with Him—took it with His hand and returned it back to its place in the soldier's head, and it became immediately as sound as it was before; and then He said to Simon: "Put up the sword into the sheath. He who draws the sword shall be killed with the sword."[2] In this He referred to the sword-drawers of His nation and His followers, but He referred to the Muslim Dispensation when He ordered His disciples to sell their garments in order to buy swords; and swords are not bought except for the sake of unsheathing them and striking with them.

[1] Luk. xxii. 35-36.

[2] Matth. xxvi. 51-52; Joh. xviii. 10-11; Luk. xxii. 50-51.

And Paul, the foremost among the Christians, whom they call an apostle, said in his Epistle to the Galatians: "Abraham had two sons, the one by a bond-maid, the other by a free-woman. But he who was of the bond-woman was like other people, but he of the free-woman was by promise from God. Both are an allegory for the two laws and covenants. Hagar is compared with Mount Sinai, which is in Arabia, and answereth to Jerusalem which now is. But Jerusalem, which is in heaven, answereth to his free wife."[1] Paul has settled many points by this saying. The *first* is that Ishmael and Hagar had inhabited the country of the Arabs, which he called the countries of Arabia; the *second* is that Mount Sinai, which is in Syria, extends and links up with the desert countries, since he says that Hagar is compared with Mount Sinai, which is in the countries of Arabia; and Sinai is the mountain mentioned in the Torah at the beginning of these prophecies: "The Lord came from Sinai, and rose up from Seir, and appeared from Mount Paran."[2] In this Paul testified that the Lord, who according to the saying of the Torah, came from Sinai, was the Prophet—may God bless and save him—and that it was he who appeared in the countries of Arabia. We have demonstrated above that the meaning of the word "Lord" refers to "prophets" and to "lords." What would be clearer and more distinct than the mention by name of the countries of Arabia? He meant by this vocable the country of the Arabs, but he wrote it in a foreign and unnatural manner, *Arab* instead of *'Arab.*[3]

The *third* meaning is that Jerusalem answers to Maccah; and the *fourth* is that this second law and this second covenant are, without any doubt, from heaven. Paul called both of them by one name, and did not dis-

[1] Gal. iv. 22-26. [2] Deut. xxxiii. 2. Cf. supra p. 86.

[3] The author refers to the Syriac version where, curiously enough, the word is written in the Greek way without the strong guttural at the beginning.

tinguish between them in any way. As to the supremacy that he gave to the free-woman, and to his saying that the son of the bond-woman was not born by promise, it is one-sidedness and prejudice on his part, because in the convincing passages of the Torah about Ishmael, which I have quoted above, there is sufficient evidence to show that he also was born, not only by one promise, but by several promises.

These are clear prophecies and established facts, perpetuated throughout the ages, which, if somebody apart from the Muslims claims, his only gain will be the deadliest arrow and the greatest lie; this will only be done by a wretched Jew or a babbling Christian, excusing with it themselves, and deceiving themselves and others. It is indeed evident to the Christians especially, and to the Jews generally, that God has intensified His wrath against the Children of Israel, has cursed them, forsaken them and their religion, and told them that He will burn the stem from which they multiplied, destroy the mass of them, and plant others in the desert and in the waste and dry land. On this subject, how great is my amazement at the Jews, who avow all these things and do not go beyond contemplating them, and burden themselves with claims through which they become full of illusion and deception. To this the Christians bear witness by their evidence against the Jews, morning and evening, that God has completely destroyed them, erased their traces from the register of the earth, and annihilated the image of their nation.

As to the community of the Christ—peace be with Him—they have no right to claim all the prophecies that I have succinctly quoted about the Prophet—may God bless and save him. They cannot claim to have made kings captives, to have enslaved princes and conducted them linked together with bonds and fetters, to have inherited desert and waste lands, to have beheaded people, to have multiplied killing and havoc in the earth, and other peculiarities which are fitting and due only to Ishmael and Hagar and their descendants, and to Maccah and its pilgrims.

Moreover, many prophets have distinctly mentioned by name the Prophet—may God bless and save him—have described him with his sword-bearers and archers, and told that death and rapacious birds shall go before his armies, and that his country shall be overcrowded with numerous caravans of camels and files of animals, and that he shall destroy the nations and the kings opposing him. All these confirm his religion, enhance his rank, and testify to the veracity of what his messengers have told about him. This is especially the case with Daniel, who closed all the prophecies with something that expels every doubt, and this is that the God of heaven will set up an everlasting kingdom which shall not change and perish. He who does not submit to him that God has chosen and raised is to be scorned and despised.

XXIX.

THE ANSWER TO THOSE WHO HAVE SAID THAT THE "REFUGEES" AND THE "HELPERS" EMBRACED THE FAITH WITHOUT ANY SIGN.

SOMEBODY might say something similar to what was used as an argument by an uncle of mine renowned for his ability in discussion and for the superiority of his intelligence, and known in the regions of 'Irāḳ and Khurāsān by the name of Abu Zakkār Yaḥya ibn-Nu'mān. In one of the books that he wrote: *Answer to Adherents to Religions*,[1] he declared that he examined the reasons why many *Refugees* and first disciples, both men and women, embraced Islām, and he did not find anyone who adhered to it by reason of a sign that he had seen or a miracle that he could report. This was a strong objection against Islām for me also, and I did not cease to be deceived and fascinated by it, until I seceded from his faith; I found then that the answer to it was easy, and the outlet from it broad. Indeed, if we retort with the same argument against them, a statement will be credited to us, which if they were to destroy, the prophecies of many of their prophets would also be destroyed. The entry of some people into the religion of a prophet without having seen a miracle from him is not something which would make vain all the other miracles of that prophet, nor is the abstention of a prophet from showing a sign on a given occasion something which would give him the lie.

The prophet Ezekiel—peace be with him—says in the tenth chapter that a company from the children of Israel came to him to test him, and to ask him some questions. The answer that Ezekiel gave them was: "God has told

[1] This book seems to be lost.

me, and has ordered me to tell you, that the Lord of Lords says: I swear by My name that I am the living one, and that I shall not give any answer to what you are asking."[1]

As to the Christ—peace be with Him—a great crowd followed Him and believed in Him without having seen any sign from Him. About this there is the saying of the evangelist Matthew, found in the fourth chapter of his Gospel, to the effect that when the Christ—peace be with Him—"was walking by the shore of the sea of Galilee, He saw two brethren, one of them was Simon whom He called Cephas—to whom He gave the direction of the affairs of His nation, and whom He constituted the foundation of His religion—and Andrew, his brother, fishing in the sea. He made a sign to them and said to them: "Follow Me, and I will make you after this day fishers of men; and they forthwith left their nets and followed Him."[2] And Matthew said in this chapter that the Christ "going on from thence, saw other two brethren, James the son of Zebedee, and John, fishing with their father; He called them to His faith, and they left their father and followed Him."[3] And Matthew said in this chapter that when the Christ "passed forth from thence, He saw a publican called Matthew, and said unto him: Follow Me; and he went with Him."[4] He means his own self, because he is the evangelist Matthew, one of the four who wrote the Gospel.

These are five from the heads, the foremost, and the earliest of the twelve Apostles, and the Gospel declares that they followed the Christ without having seen any sign and heard any convincing word from Him, apart from a mere call. Would that I knew what harm has come to the Christ from that, or what has shocked my uncle Abu Zakkār and those who subscribe to his opinion, from the fact that those who followed the Prophet—may

[1] Ezek. xx. 1-3.
[2] Matth. iv. 18-20.
[3] Matth. iv. 21-22.
[4] Matth. ix. 9.

God bless and save him—did so without having seen a sign from him. If what we have mentioned necessarily annuls the remaining miracles of the Christ—peace be with Him—it is then that the signs of the Prophet—may God bless and save him—will necessarily be annulled, on the ground that those who embraced his religion did so without having seen a sign from him.

Some people came to the Christ—peace be with Him—asking Him for a sign; and He not only did not show them any sign, but rebuked them strongly and reproved them with their generations. The evangelist Matthew bears witness to that, in the twelfth chapter, and tells that a company of the Jews came to the Christ and asked Him for a sign, but He answered them and said: "The evil and adulterous generation seeketh after a sign; and there shall be no sign given to it, but the sign of the prophet Jonas."[1] He told them that He would not show them a sign at all, because they were from the evil generation, meaning by that all the race of the Jews. As to the sign of Jonas which He mentioned, it is his three-days stay in the whale's belly; further, this is not one of the prophecies of the Christ, but it is one of the signs of Jonas; and Jonas was a long period of time before Him. A sign consists in wonders that a prophet shows to onlookers, which nobody besides him is able to perform; or in his prophesying about things hidden from him, which are realised in his time.

If somebody says: "My sign is that Moses rent the sea, and the Christ quickened a dead man," it will not be accepted from him, because this is an argument in favour of another one, and not of himself; however, no one can think of the Christ that He was short of answers, nor that He contradicted Himself, nor that He promised something from which He afterwards desisted, nor that He said that He would not do something which He did. His saying, therefore, to those of the Children of Israel

[1] Matth. xii. 39.

who had asked Him for a sign, that there would be no answer to their demand, emanates either from God or from Himself; if it emanates from God, God then did the contrary of what He said to them, because He showed them signs at the hands of the Christ, after this event: and if it emanates from Himself, then the Christ also did the contrary of what He said, and disagreed with His first saying; and this does not suit Him, and is inconceivable of somebody like Him. As to me, I count this also as an alteration and corruption in the text of the Gospel, by translators and copyists.

And Matthew said in the sixteenth chapter that when the Jews saw the Christ calling people and turning them away from Judaism, they gathered to Him and said: "By what authority doest thou what we see, and who gave thee this authority?" In answer to them Jesus said: "I also will ask you one thing, which if ye tell Me, I in like wise will tell you about your question. Tell Me about the baptism of John, son of Zacharias, whence was it? From heaven, or from earth?" The crowd abstained from answering, and said "We do not know;" and the Christ said "Neither tell I you by what authority I work."[1] We do not see that He answered the crowd about what they had asked Him, but He simply competed with them by propounding another question to them; and no one was able to find fault with Him on this account.

And Matthew said in the sixth[2] chapter that Pilate, the representative of the King of the Romans, said to the Christ, when the Jews brought Him to him: "I adjure thee by the truth of God to tell me: art thou the Christ, son of God, or not?" And the Christ—peace be with Him—did not say to him more than "Thou hast said."[3] There is neither affirmation nor negation in this saying, and one is allowed to say that He meant to dispel and discard this attribution from Himself, and to rebuke

[1] Matth. xxi. 23-28. [2] *Sic* Cod. [3] Matth. xxvi. 63-64.

those who ascribed it to Him; if not, why did He not say "I am the son of God," when He was asked? And why did He not show a sign to clear up the question, and put the Jews to shame and confusion? This also is a question to which the Christ gave no answer, and it has not prejudiced the dignity of His rank nor His previous signs.

And it is said in the Gospel which is in the hands of the Christians that the Jews said to the Christ: "If thou be the son of God, come down from the cross, that we may believe in Thee;"[1] and He did not do it, nor did He show any sign; and we do not say, because of this, that He had no previous sign; indeed He foresaw more than anybody else the issues of this question, and what God wanted from Him, or had determined for Him.

More forceful is what Matthew said in the second chapter, that Satan said to the Christ when he was tempting Him: "If thou be the son of God, direct these stones to become bread;" and the Christ did not say to him more than: "It is written in the Books of Revelation that man shall not live by bread alone, but by every word that proceedeth out of the mouth of God."[2]

Do you not see—may God guide you—that the Christ—peace be with Him—and other prophets were asked questions to which they gave no answers, and were requested to perform miracles which they did not perform, because God had not permitted them to act otherwise and had not opened to them at the moment the doors of miracles? And the disciples asked the Christ—peace be with Him—about the Hour; and He said: "This is a secret and a hidden thing from Me, which God alone knoweth."[3] Since this has not been a cause of blame and reprobation to the Christ, it likewise must not be for the Prophet—may God bless and save him.

These are convincing and fair replies and answers,

[1] Matth. xxvii. 40, etc. [2] Matth. iv. 3-4.
[3] Matth. xxiv. 36, etc.

and cogent arguments, to that proposition and contention to which the disciples of my uncle Abu Zakkār and those who subscribe to his opinion, cling. I did not find a single Christian scholar, either in ancient or in modern times, who argued with this point against the Muslims, except my uncle; but God has refuted and explained it by His grace and favour, and by the wisdom, the replies, and the good suggestions of the Commander of the Faithful—may God strengthen him—and by what I profited by them.

Now exercise your mind—may God guide you—and let not your intelligence be idle; know that you have been created for a great task, and that you are standing at the brink of heaven or of Fire; he with whom this brink crumbles away into Fire[1] shall be in the abyss of everlasting shame, eternal regret and torment, which the Christ—peace be with Him—has described as a fire which is not quenched, and as worms which do not die;[2] but he whom truth takes up to the courts of heaven and to the altitudes of the heavenly Gardens, shall be happy and a winner of a great victory, and shall possess eternal peace and happiness, which no eye has seen and of which no ear has heard. Give, therefore, good advice to your souls, and do not deceive them; be true to them, and do not beguile them. Truth has become clear, the hiding veil has been withdrawn, and evidence has become manifest.

[1] Ḳur. ix. 110.

[2] Mark, ix. 44, etc.

XXX.

THE ANSWER TO THOSE WHO HAVE BLAMED ISLĀM IN ONE OF ITS PRACTICES OR IN ONE OF ITS PRESCRIPTIONS.

If a man from the *People of the Book* reviles one of the rules of the faith, and one of the practices of the Muslims, he will be grossly unjust to us, will repudiate and blame all the prophets, and will expose himself to sin and punishment. If they blame sacrifices, they are inherited from Abraham and from all the prophets of his posterity—peace be with them. If they reprobate circumcision, it was practised by the Christ and by those who preceded Him. If they condemn divorce, their own Books will render their endeavour fruitless; and if they condemn swearing by God, it is the saying of the Most High to His prophets;[1] the prophet Isaiah—peace be with him—declared on behalf of God: "I drew the permanent word out of My mouth, that unto Me every knee shall bow, and by Me every tongue shall swear."[2] And Paul, whom the Christians call an apostle, said that God made His promises to Abraham, in his seed, and swore to him by Himself.[3] And Daniel said that the angel who appeared to him lifted his hand to heaven and swore by the Eternal Merciful that all that he had said would surely take place.[4]

If they blame the Holy War, Abraham fought the four kings who had made inroads into the country of Jazīrah to invade its inhabitants; he protected his neighbours and the people with whom he was living,

[1] One line of the text is much damaged here, and some words have only been conjectured.

[2] Isa. xlv. 23. [3] Cf. Galat. iii. 16. [4] Cf. Dan. xii. 7.

destroyed the armies of the enemy with his servants and men born in his house, and won from this fact honour, credit, eternal remembrance, and perpetual praise; he gave back to their respective kings all the booty and the men he saved, and did not hold back anything from the spoils, not even a bead or a utensil, after these kings had abandoned their countries and surrendered them.[1]

And Joshua, son of Nun, killed thirty-one kings from the kings of Syria,[2] and did not leave in one of their towns called 'Ani[3] a single dweller, nor a man to blow the fire; and he did not call them to religion, nor did he require tribute and capitation from them, nor did he receive ransom from them, as the Muslims do.

And the prophet Samuel—peace be with him—said in the twelfth chapter that the prophet David—peace be with him—raided a Syrian country called Philistia, and did not leave there a single man nor a single woman without killing them. He then took sheep, cattle, asses, and camels, and swept away with him goods, treasures, and furniture, without calling the inhabitants either to religion, or to pay tribute, or to submit.[4] And the Book of Samuel relates that David was hungry one day, and sent his retainers to a certain man in search of food, and they did not bring him anything. He then went with his men to attack this man and the inhabitants of his village; but behold, he saw the man's wife coming to meet him, bringing him food and wine, for fear that he should punish her husband.[5] He accepted that from her, and was satisfied; and his wrath cooled down and left him. This and similar deeds of prophets are neither reprobated nor blamed.

As to the Prophet—may God bless and save him—he ordered, with persuasion and dissuasion, to worship One, Eternal, and Omnipotent God, in order that religion

[1] Cf. Gen. xiv. 5 seq.

[2] Josh. xii. 24.

[3] Probably '*Ai* (cf. Josh. viii. 1 seq.).

[4] Cf. 1 Sam. xxvii. 8 seq.

[5] Cf. 1 Sam. xxv. 2-36.

might be One and the Supreme Being One. He who responds to that has the prerogatives and the obligations of the Muslims; and he who does not respond but gives tribute on his hand in an humble condition,[1] he spares his blood with this tribute and upon his submission has a right to the compact of protection. This point constitutes a fine subject of meditation for the unbelievers; indeed, it lowers their amour-propre and their pride, and calls the people of honour and self-esteem among them to change their state of lowliness, and their compact of protection by means of tribute, for the glory of dignity and freedom. If they are averse to tribute and submission, war shall be behind them.

And Moses—peace be with him—did more than that. When he ordered the Children of Israel to leave Egypt and go away, he told them that the Most High God had ordered that every one of them should borrow the garments of his neighbour and acquaintance and the jewels of their wives and daughters, and that they should inform them that it was for the occasion of one of their feasts. The Egyptian people yielded to this, adorned the Israelites with what they had, and lent them both their useful and necessary things. The Children of Israel numbered then about six hundred thousand combatants. When all was gathered to them and was in their possession, they journeyed all the night and departed one and all. And God rent the sea for them, and they crossed it; Pharaoh sought after them, and they dreaded him, but God drowned Pharaoh, and set the heart of the Israelites at rest from him.[2] The owners of those borrowed objects, and their wives and daughters were deprived of their loaned articles; and their treasures, a griffin carried them away;[3] and they bit their fingers out of regret.

All this was not unlawful and illicit, but was simply the right of booty and spoils; for the world belongs to

[1] Ḳur. ix. 29. [2] Cf. Exod. xi. 2; xii. 35-37, etc.

[3] A proverb meaning "that they would not see them again."

the Most High God, and its Kingdom and ornaments belong to those of His servants upon whom He bestows them, as He said in His Book: "Thou givest the Kingdom to whomsoever Thou pleasest, and strippest the Kingdom from whomsoever Thou pleasest."[1] And inasmuch as what was done by the prophets whom we have mentioned is not shameful and sinful, but as something done by way of tacit authorisation and good-will of God,[2] so also are to be considered the holy war against the polytheists and the attacks against the unbelievers, the injunction of which God laid upon the Prophet—may God bless and save him. Without holy war no religion could stand, no inviolable thing could be safe, no gap could be filled, and the Muslims would become the prey and possession of their enemies. Men would scarcely remain in a religion with such standing without passing to what is higher and safer.

The Christ—peace be with Him—had forbidden war and given warning against its causes in saying: "Whosoever shall compel thee to go a mile, go with him twain; whosoever taketh away thy coat, give him thy cloak also; whosoever shall smite thee on thy cheek, turn to him the other also."[3] By this order the Christ—peace be with Him—left but little spiritual and temporal power to His followers, and transferred their heritage to the members of another nation who stirred war in East and West, and kindled it with spears and swords as far as the countries of the Greeks, of the Franks, of the tent-dwelling Turanians,[4] and of the Armenians. Outside these countries what Christians are to be found in the country

[1] Ḳur. iii. 25. [2] Ḳur. lvii. 20.

[3] Matth. v. 39-40; Luk. vi. 29.

[4] This is probably the earliest mention made of the Turanians in any Christian or Islamic work. See *A Manual on the Turanians and Turanianism*, London, 1918, pp. 12-14. The author appears to believe that at least a great number of the Turanian Turks were Christian in his time, and seems to imply that *Turanian* is not absolutely identical with *Turk*. The habitat of the Turanians was probably not very far from Mongolia.

of the Turks except a small and despicable quantity of Nestorians scattered among the nations? or what are those found among the Arabs except a sprinkling of Jacobites and Melchites?

Then we have seen that the Christ—peace be with Him—gave permission ultimately to take swords; and in that he abrogated the first order. He said, indeed, to His disciples: "Let each one of you sell his garment and buy a sword with it for himself"[1] And He said: "Think not I am come to sow peace on earth, but war."[2] He who slurs Islâm in what has been considered good, and put in practice, by the prophets whom we have mentioned, deviates from the path of justice.

If somebody reprobates the saying of the Prophet—may God bless and save him,—that in the world to come there is food and drink, the answer would be that the Christ—peace be with Him—declared also such a thing to His disciples when He drank with them and said to them: "I will not drink of this fruit of the vine, until I drink it another time with you in the kingdom of heaven."[3] In this He declared that in heaven there is wine and drink; and where drink is found, food and pleasures are not blamed. And Luke declares in his Gospel that the Christ—peace be with Him—said: "You shall eat and drink at the table of my Father."[4] And John declares that the Christ—peace be with Him—said: "There are many mansions and dwellings at my Father's."[5]

All these confirm the existence of food and drink in the world to come, and of mansions and pleasures, according to what the Most High God said in His Book: "And gardens shall they have therein and lasting pleasure."[6]

[1] Luk. xxii. 36 (cf. supra, p. 143).
[2] Matth. x. 34.
[3] Matth. xxvi. 29.
[4] Luk. xxii. 30.
[5] Joh. xiv. 2.
[6] Ḳur. ix. 21.

XXXI.

THE ANSWER TO THOSE WHO REPROBATE THE FACT THAT THE PROPHET—MAY GOD BLESS AND SAVE HIM—CONTRADICTED MOSES AND CHRIST—PEACE BE WITH BOTH OF THEM—IN CHANGING THE RULES OF THE TORAH AND THE GOSPEL.

If one of those adversaries who penetrate deeply into science contends that the Prophet—may God bless and save him—believed in the Torah and the Gospel in his words, but disagreed with them in his actions, and that in the fact of his confirming them once and contradicting them another time there are in him indications of inconsistency, we will reply that God—may He be blessed and exalted—is Wise, Knower, Compassionate, Merciful; creatures are for Him, guidance is from Him, power and strength are by Him; and His servants are not to object to what He does, nor to interfere with His prescience and the secrets of His Providence, but they should submit and obey.

The most High God said through Moses—peace be with him—"God will raise you up a prophet from amongst your brethren, like unto me; hearken unto him; and he who does not hearken unto him, I will avenge myself on him."[1] The Prophet—peace be with him—appeared from amongst the brethren of the Jews, followed the prescriptions of God, and believed in Moses, of whom he said that "he conversed with God,"[2] and believed also in Jesus, of whom he said that He was "The Spirit of God and His Word, whom He has chosen, honoured, and taken to heaven; and He is with Him;"[3]

[1] Deut. xviii. 18-19 (cf. supra, p. 85).
[2] Ḳur. iv. 164, etc.
[3] Ḳur. iv. 156, 169, etc.

and he did not contradict Moses in the article of the unity of God, nor did he utter on this subject ambiguities and equivocations as the Christians did, but he openly and clearly proclaimed it, and rendered faith pure and his saying precise. Moreover, all the prophets agreed with him with regard to the *Ḳiblah*, divorce, circumcision, fight against the unbelievers, protection of children by forcible means, and retaliation. And he multiplied sacrifices to the Most High God alone, and renewed to his nation rules and prescriptions which tally with the order of God; and the servants of God have nothing left to them but to obey God through him.

If people were permitted to slight and reprobate divine orders and economy of this kind, one would be allowed to say about the Christ that He once believed in the Torah and said: "I am not come to destroy it, but to fulfil it; verily, I say unto you, Till heaven and earth pass, one letter shall not pass from it,"[1] and then He openly contradicted Moses, and flung the Torah aside, to such an extent that the learned men of His community have reason to say openly and publicly: "The Old Testament has passed and gone, and the New Testament has come and appeared;[2] they mean by Old Testament the Torah and its laws and the other Books of the prophets, and by New Testament the Gospel and the Books of the Apostles. As to the pillar of the Torah—the prop of Judaism—its rites, its circumcision, its sacrifices, its feasts, its law of retaliation, its decisions, its priesthood, and its altars, the Christ—peace be with Him—has abrogated and annulled all of them. He did not leave the Jews a feast, without abolishing it; a Sabbath, without infringing it; a circumcision, without gently rejecting it; a sacrifice, without forbidding it; an altar, without despoiling it; and a priest, without calling him adulterous and profligate.

[1] Matth. v. 17-18.

[2] This thought is frequently found in the East Syrian or Nestorian Breviary.

Matthew said in the thirteenth chapter that the Christ—peace be with Him—"went on the Sabbath day through the cornfields, and His disciples were an-hungred, and began to pluck the ears of corn and to eat;"[1] and He did not blame their action, nor did He reprobate it. And Matthew said in this chapter[2] that the Christ, pointing to the Children of Israel who were present with Him, said: "You have heard the Torah say, Whosoever shall put away his wife, let him give her a writing of divorcement; but I say unto you that whosoever shall put away his wife, saving for the cause of fornication, causeth her to commit adultery, and whosoever shall marry a divorced woman shall commit adultery."[3] One might say, in disapprobation of this saying: What has a husband to do with a wife who committed sorcery, or became infidel, or poisoned her parents, or killed her child, or had intercourse with him? Can he not divorce her for all these? But how? That would be impossible for him, because the Christ has permitted divorce only in case of adultery.

And He said in this chapter: "You have heard that it has been said in the Books of Revelation: A tooth for a tooth, and an eye for an eye; but I say unto you: Whosoever shall smite thee on thy cheek, turn to him the other cheek also, and whosoever shall ask thee, refuse him not."[4] And Paul, who has the precedence among them, and whom they obey, said: "Circumcision is nothing, and uncircumcision is nothing."[5] In this he openly abolished circumcision. This and similar things are not considered blameable and reprehensible on the part of Christ—may God bless and save Him—; similarly, the new rules, the additions to, and the subtractions from, the rules of the Torah and the Gospel, which the Prophet—may God bless and save him—has innovated, are not to be reprobated and blamed.

[1] Matth. xii. 1.
[2] *Sic* Cod.
[3] Matth. v. 31-32.
[4] Matth. v. 39-40, 42.
[5] 1 Cor. vii. 19.

XXXII.

THE ANSWER TO THOSE WHO HAVE PRETENDED THAT NO ONE BUT THE CHRIST—PEACE BE WITH HIM—MENTIONED THE RESURRECTION.

THE Christians have said that nobody but the Christ has made known the Resurrection, and proclaimed the Last Day and the Revivification. By my life, He has proclaimed it and announced it in clear words, and God has honoured Him with an honour greater than that of His predecessors; but the prophets who preceded Him knew it and mentioned it. The prophet Moses said on behalf of God: "I am alone, and there is no God besides Me; I kill and I make alive."[1] And the prophet David said in the Psalter: "The giants shall be resuscitated and revivified, and they shall glorify Thee, O Lord, and they shall declare that Thy grace is in the graves."[2] And God—may He be blessed and exalted—said also through him: "I will revivify them and resuscitate them from the teeth of the lions and from the depths of the sea."[3] And the prophet Daniel—peace be with Him—said: "A great multitude shall be resuscitated from the graves, some to everlasting life, and some to perdition and to the contempt of their companions for ever."[4] And Hannah the prophetess—peace be with her—said in the Book of the prophet Samuel—peace be with him—"The Lord killeth and maketh alive; He bringeth down to the grave, and bringeth up from it."[5] And the Most High God said to Daniel—peace be with him—"Go and lie down (in conformity with) the decreed order; and thou shalt rise, at the appointed moment, at the end of the world."[6]

[1] Deut. xxxii. 39. [2] Ps. lxxxviii. 10. [3] Ps. lxviii. 22
[4] Dan. xii. 2. [5] I. Sam. ii. 6. [6] Dan. xii. 13.

XXXIII.

CONCLUSION.

Now that you know—may God guide you—that our common agreement is in accordance with your common agreement on the point that God is just, that He loves justice and those who practise it, and that He has forbidden injustice and iniquity, it is just and fair that you should look back into the motives for which you have accepted your religion and see what they are. If it becomes evident to you that they are only possible and praiseworthy stories transmitted to you by a successor from his predecessor, and by a last from a first man, it is also through such stories that we have accepted the Prophet—peace be with him.

Moreover, among those who handed down to you those stories of yours, there was none who claimed that he had taken them from an eye-witness among his fathers or grandfathers who had seen the Christ or Moses—peace be with them—as the Arabs claim on the authority of their fathers and their grandfathers who had seen the Prophet—peace be with him. Indeed, a man among the Arabs records, on the authority of his grandfather or the grandfather of his grandfather, or a man of his relatives, what they have seen and transmitted to their successors. As to your stories, they have been handed down to you by a man of 'Irāḳ, who took them from a man of Jazīrah, who in his turn took them from a man of Syria, who himself took them from an Hebrew; or by a Persian, who took them from a Greek; or by an Eastern, who took them from a Western, through obscure and irregular channels. How, then, could you refute or blame the man who says: "I have accepted this religion of Islām and believed in it by means of the evidences and testimonies through which you have accepted your own religion?"; or who says: "When I saw members of a nation great in rank and high in dignity with regard to number, power, piety, wisdom, and uprightness, telling me what we have related above, as having heard it from their fathers and grandfathers, and showing a Book they transmit to one another, century after century, which calls to the unity of God and His glorification and to the belief in His apostles and prophets; which refuses to acknowledge associates and equals with God; which enjoins the best and highest things and that which is in harmony with the rules and the recommendations of the prophets; which warns its adherents against evil and evildoers; and which foretells events, which were realised time after time and year after year; then, when I found that the Books of those of the prophets in whom you believe had testified to our Prophet and prophesied about his empire and his religion as we have already demonstrated—I embraced such a religion, and hoped for what, through it, I shall have with God."

If you pretend that there is no obligation to acknowledge the man of such description, prophetic office, merits, and evidences, all that you yourself claim will be abolished, and with all your belief you will be thrown into unbelief. And if you excuse yourself with reference to Dualists and Pagans and the like, that they also transmit stories from their religious leaders, and relate wonders of their messengers and deceivers, and prove the veracity of their stories from their own religious books and written histories—we have already spoken of that, at the beginning of this book, with such evidence that the only men who would close their ears to it would be those whose only aim is to quibble and to refrain from serious discussion, and whose only religion is obstinacy and arrogance; such false leaders, because they have contradicted themselves and have called men to impurity and aberration, have gone astray, and because they have associated other gods with God, have run to perdition. Such men are not to be compared with a man whose leader was truth, whose aim was true guidance, whose distinctive mark was devotion and asceticism, and whose call was to One and Unique God, the God of Abraham and of the rest of the prophets—peace be with them—and about whom the prophets had prophesied in terms which are now quite obvious.

Waive, therefore, suspicions and excuses, O my cousins—may God guide you—and walk in the safest and most direct way, and avoid the most misleading and crooked path. If you ponder well, it will become evident to you that the motives and reasons for which we have accepted the prophetic office of the Prophet—peace be with him—are similar to the motives and the reasons for which you have accepted Christ and Moses—peace be with both of them; therefore, if we are wrong and exposed to the punishment of God, so also are you. Discuss, therefore, with your own souls, summon us to the tribunal of your mind and intelligence, and argue for us and for yourselves, against us and against yourselves, in order that the veil may be withdrawn from you; you will then, by the assistance of God, see the truth itself.

If somebody blames the Prophet—peace be with him—and says that he—peace be with him—attributed evil to God, the answer is that he has pronounced clear statements about the justice, mercy, and might of God; and these we have mentioned at the beginning of this book. And God—may He be blessed and exalted—said to Moses—peace be with him—"I will harden Pharaoh's heart, that he should not bring you out of the land of Egypt."[1] And the prophet Isaiah—peace be with him—said: "God hath made peace, and hath created both good and evil."[2] And Paul, who has the precedence among the Christians and whom they obey, said in his Epistle to Timothy:

[1] Exod. vii. 3-4.

[2] Isa. xlv. 7.

"In a great house there are not only vessels of silver and gold, but also vessels of wood and of earth; some to honour and some to dishonour."[1] He means by that the world, and all the happy and wretched people who are in it.

At the end of this book I will ask you—may God guide you—a general, decisive, and convincing question. What would you say of a man coming to this country from the regions of India and China, with the intention of being rightly guided, of inquiring into the religions found in it, and of acquainting himself with the customs of its inhabitants?

It will be said to him that some of its inhabitants belong to a religion called *Magianism*. They worship stars and fires, and pretend that God is the creator of good and light, and that Satan is the creator of darkness and evil; that war is never at rest between them, and because they do not obtain their desire, they have neither peace nor respite, and are powerless and bewildered; that the will of God and His pleasure are that one should have intercourse with one's mother and daughter, purify himself with the rotten fluid excretion of cows, and cleave to immoral converse and dance; that the spirits of their dead come back to them once a year, partake of the food and drink put before them, and at their withdrawal provision themselves;[2] and they have some other vicious and occult customs similar to those we have mentioned at the beginning of this book, with filthy habits, and clear signs of vengeance from God on them, and ancient prophecies against them, found in the Books of the prophets, to which we have referred above.

Some of its inhabitants belong to a religion called *Zindiḳism*. Their religion is similar to that of the Magians, and it goes even in advance of it in error, perverseness, filth, impurity, and stupidity.

[1] II. Tim. ii. 20.

[2] This information is not without historical interest.

Some of its inhabitants belong to a religion called *Christianism.* A branch of them pretend that when God saw that the power of Satan was becoming supreme and its strength formidable, and that the prophets were unable to resist him, He found for Himself an eternal and everlasting Son, not rivalled by any creature, who entered into the womb of a woman, and was born of her; then He grew up and strove with Satan; but Satan seized Him, killed Him, and then crucified Him at the hands of a band of his followers.[1] Another branch of them assume that the One who was killed was only the temple and the habitation of that Son, with whom He had become so united that this eternal Son ate the same food as that of the created, went to the place of easement with Him, and was killed with Him.[2]

Some of its inhabitants belong to a religion called *Judaism.* They have in their hands Books of some men whom they call prophets, and relate how these prophets have cursed them, and report that God has completely forsaken them, execrated their religion, scattered them in all regions, extinguished their light, and sworn that He will never pity them again.

Some of its inhabitants belong to this pure and sublime religion called *Islām.* They say that God is One, Eternal, who has no partner with Him, and whom no one can overcome, because to Him belong omnipotence and everlastingness. He has no child and no father, and He is the Compassionate, the Merciful, the First, and the Last. Their Prophet has prescribed, on behalf of God, piety to parents, fasting, prayer, purity, and cleanliness; has made lawful for them the good things, and forbidden the evil things, and has promised heaven, and warned against Fire.

In which of these religions and creeds would that Indian or that Chinese wish to believe, and to which of

[1] Allusion to the Jacobites. [2] Allusion to the Nestorians.

them would he incline, and of which of them would he approve, if he were a man of broad mind, sound judgment, and an enquirer after mere truth and nothing else?

And what would be the argument of God against any one of His servants who would say to Him, Just and Compassionate as He is, who does not wrong anybody by the weight of an atom:[1]

"I heard a preacher call to Thy Unity, magnify Thee, praise Thee, and glorify Thee; and I responded to him. I heard[2] him order us to believe in Thy prophets and in Thy Chosen Ones, and prescribe prayer, fasting, and alms; and I obeyed him, in the hope of the reward which I shall have with Thee, and in obedience to Thy order. I heard him urge us to go on pilgrimage to a far and remote country; and I made this pilgrimage, and did not hesitate. I heard him exhort us to wage war against Thy enemies who disbelieve in Thee, and do not pray to Thee; and I prayed to Thee and fought a holy war, with all my might and not half-heartedly, wishing in all things to please Thee. I saw disgraceful and occult religions and creeds—such as those I have mentioned above—and I cast them aside, left them completely, and held to what I thought was the most solid handle, and the best way to please Thee. O my God, if I have mistaken what I have chosen, and have erred in what I have selected, Thou hast the strongest reason to pity Thy servant who exerted his utmost in the search of what is with Thee, but mistook the way to come to Thee."

O my cousins, this is an acceptable saying, and not a despicable excuse, even with the imperfect and exacting servants of God; how much more so then with the Most Compassionate of the merciful, and the most equitable judge who does not require of a soul more than its capacity?

[1] Cf. Ḳur. iv. 44, etc. [2] Lit. "I saw".

Examine then—may God guide you—these arguments and illustrations, throw away mischievous prejudices, and remove the veil from your eyes and the covers and the locks from your hearts; content yourselves, in the chapters that I have written, either with the one which deals with the prophetic office, or with the one concerning the stories related of the Prophet—peace be with him—or with the one relating to the resplendent victory won in the name of the God of Abraham; or with the one on the living Book of the Kur'ān and its merits, which I have set forth above; or with the one on the successive prophecies of the prophets, and the meanings and interpretations that I have given to them. Listen to my advice, because I have sifted for you my admonitions, and know that I have sought in what I have written neither vain glory nor distinction, but only what is with God who does not disappoint the man who trusts in Him, and in compliance with the wish of His Caliph and servant Ja'far al-Mutawakkil 'ala Allah, the Commander of the Faithful—may God strengthen him.

I expect gratitude and ask for consideration from pious and magnanimous Muslims, and also from the more intelligent and able men among the members of the protected cults, since I have demonstrated to the common people among them what I have thoroughly investigated, and disclosed to them what I know with certitude, and made them understand what I had myself understood, intending by that that they should participate in the light brought to me, and in the final success for which I hope. In case I am right in what I have said my merit and my success should redound on me and on them, and in case I am wrong the blame should be laid on me to the exclusion of them. I crave the continuation of Divine protection and assistance, and I take refuge with God from my want of requisite knowledge, in beseeching Him to remove scandal, and to grant me the garment of modesty and righteousness, and the attainment of what sooner or later I hoped from Him, in what I have written and said.

This my book, which I have entitled *Book of Religion and Empire*,[1] has decisively demonstrated the unsoundness and fallacy of Judaism, the villainy and falseness of Dualism and Atheism,[2] and the onlooker already observes their downfall and their eclipse, and sees that resplendent light and true faith are exclusively in Islām.

I first thank God for His guidance to me, then His servant and Caliph Ja'far al-Mutawakkil 'ala Allah, Commander of the Faithful—may God prolong his life—who invited and attracted me to him, along with other people of the protected cults, by persuasion and dissuasion, and by the respect and consideration that he has for all. It is for this reason that I devoted the first chapter of this book to a description of what my community has experienced from his munificence, from the tokens of his mercy, the gentleness of his administration, the prosperity of his reign, and the great number of his conquests, and to show the obligation of Muslims and non-Muslims alike to love him, to obey him, and to be grateful to him.

Peace be with those who follow true guidance, who befriend piety, who love righteousness and virtue, who seek partisans for them, and who exhort to them!

[1] *Kitāb ud-Din wa'd-Daulah.*

[2] More especially the doctrine of the eternity of matter.

THE END.

INDEX.

A.

'Abbās, 47, 48, 126.
'Abbās (Abu), 45, 46.
'Abbās (ibn), 33.
'Abbasid, 45-46, 126, 137-138.
'Abdallah (Anṣāri), 35.
'Abdallah (b. 'Abbās), 47.
'Abdallah (b. 'Umar), 70, 72.
Abraham, 2, 20, 58, 77, 79, 80, 81, 90, 97, 102, 115, 130, 144, 153, 164, 168.
Abtaḥi, 54.
Abyssinia, 82.
Abyssinians, 39, 106.
'Ād, 72.
Adam, 7, 22, 130.
'Adi, 13, 48, 49.
Agabus, 18.
Aḥmad, 42, 99, 108, 111.
Ahwāz, 67, 126.
'Ai, 154.
Ajnādain, 48.
Alexander, 7, 58, 126.
'Ali, 25, 43, 44, 66, 69.
'Ali (the author), 1, cf. 19, 50, 147, 169.
Aminah, 32.
'Ammār, 43.
Anas, 32, 34, 35, 44.
Andrew, 148.
'Ansi (the liar), 47.
Antioch, 18.
Arab, 3, 34, 41, 49, 50, 57, 84, 87, 91, 98, 113, 114, 116, 125, 127, 137, 144, 157, 162.
Arabia, 99, 103, 144.
Arabic, 105, 121, 122, 130, 142.
Ardashir, 58.
Armenians, 156.
'Ās, 31.
Ashimun, 104.
Aswad (b. Muṭṭalib), 31.
Aswad (b. 'Abd Yaghūth), 31.
Atheists, 58, 169.
'Āyeshah, 25, 43, 55.

B.

Babylon, 96, 97, 126, 127, 129, 137.
Badr, 32.
Baghdad, cf. 114, 127.
Bahrām, 84.
Bakr (Abu), 30, 33, 42, 45, 49, 61-64
Barḳah, 101.
Barnabas, 18.
Bashan, 93.
Baṣrah, 13, 43, 73.
Beersheba, 79.
Berbers, 114.
Bishtāsaf, 10.
Buddhists, 7, 8.

C.

Caesar, 46, 113.
Chaldaeans, 127.
China, 165.
Chinese, 7, 166.
Chosrau, 46, 49, 65, 67, 100, 113.
Christ, 12, 14, 15, 16, 17, 18, 25, 36, 51, 55, 59, 74, 75, 77, 83, 86, 96, 106, 130, 136, 137, 139, 140-143, 145, 147-152, 156-157, 158-160, 161, 162, 164.
Christian, 11, 12, 15, 17, 18, 28, 36, 50, 51, 57, 75, 76, 80, 81, 106, 120, 124, 130, 137, 139, 144, 145, 151, 153, 156, 159, 161, 164.
Christianism, 11, 82, 106.
Copt, 81.
Cyrene, 18.

D.

Damascus, 66, 126.
Daniel, 16, 133-139, 142, 146, 153, 161.
David, 16, 28, 54, 55, 86, 88-92, 93, 115, 127, 131, 154, 161.
Dualism, 11, 123, 169.
Dualists, 58, 163.
Dūmat (Jandal), 39.
Duranim, 97.

E.

Edom, 115.
Egypt, 50, 53, 76, 81, 82, 155, 164.
Egyptian, 54, 155.
Elam, 95, 125, 126, 127.
Elisha, 16.
Ephah, 110.
Euphrates, 90.
Eve, 7.
Ezekiel, 17, 53, 128-129, 133, 147.

F.

Fākhir, 13.
Fāṭimah, 25, 42, 44.
Franks, 156.

G.

Gabriel, 2, 26, 31, 80.
Galatians, 144.
Galilee, 148.
Ghifār (banu), 33.
Gihon, 90.
Gorīyah, 84.
Greek (language), 121.
Greek, 7, 48, 50, 54, 91, 98, 121, 156, 162.

H.

Habakkuk, 119, 131.
Hagar, 77, 78, 79, 80, 83, 105, 106, 107, 108, 109, 113, 114, 130, 144, 146.
Haggai, 17.
Ḥamīd, 89.
Hannah, 17, 161.
Ḥārith, 32.
Ḥarithiyah, 45.
Ḥasan, 44, 66.
Hāshimites, 73.
Ḥaw'ab, 43.
Hebrew (language), 98, 121.
Hebrew (Jew), 162.
Helpers, 48, 85, 147.
Ḥijāz, 82, 101, 103, 114.
Ḥims, 71.
Ḥīrah, 45, 48.
Hormiz, 12.
Hormizān, 67.
Hosea, 17, 53, 117.

I.

Ifriḳiyah, 101.
'Ikrimah, 48.
India, 8, 82, 114, 122, 165.
Indian, 7, 8, 50, 54, 166.
'Irāḳ, 13, 72, 101, 126, 127, 147, 162.
Iran-Shahr, 122.
Isaac, 2, 20, 58, 81, 97.
Isaiah, 16, 51, 53, 91, 93-116, 117, 124, 130, 131, 153, 164.
Ishmael, 2, 14, 20, 58, 77-84, 85, 87, 92, 94, 95, 102, 110, 115, 137, 144, 145, 146.
Islām, 1, 3, 4, 11, 18, 19, 46, 47, 49, 59, 62, 74, 102, 124, 142, 147, 157, 162, 166, 169.
Israel, 28, 29, 51, 53, 83, 85, 86, 96, 102, 103, 108, 111, 112, 113, 120, 124, 125, 130, 136, 137, 145, 147, 149, 155, 160.
Israelites, 52, 86, 155.

J.

Jābir (Anṣāri), 35.
Jacob, 2, 20, 58.
Jacobites, 157.
Jam (the King), 7.
James, 148.
Jazīrah, 153, 162.
Jeremiah, 16, 51, 124-127.
Jerusalem, 18, 53, 118, 129, 137, 144.
Jesus, 2, 28, 30, 106, 142, 158.
Jew, 12, 28, 52, 53, 59, 76, 81, 86, 124, 128, 129, 130, 142, 143, 145, 149, 150-151, 158, 159.
Jewish, 52, 78.
John, 140, 141, 142, 148, 157.
John (son of Zacharias), 117, 150.
Jonas, 149.
Joshua, 86, 154.
Judaism, 82, 150, 159, 166, 169.
Judas, 18.

K.

Ḳaḥtān, 13.
Ḳalwādha, 127.
Ḳārūn, 72.
Ḳāsim (Abu), 62.
Ḳedar, 92, 110.

Khālid (b. Walīd), 39.
Khazar, 82, 122.
Khurāsān, 45, 147.
Khuzistān, 97.
Kūfah, 73.
Ḳūmis, 13.
Ḳuraish, 38, 47.
Ḳur'ān, 15, 16, 17, 18, 20, 27, 28, 29, 30, 31, 36, 37, 38, 40, 41, 50-56, 73, 94, 101, 125, 140, 168.
Kush, 121.

L.

Lahab, 31.
Lebanon, 90, 93, 99, 111.
Lucius, 18.
Luke, 18, 55, 143, 157.

M.

Maccah, 33, 34, 39, 73, 87, 90, 107' 109, 110, 112, 113, 114, 115, 116, 118, 129, 142, 144, 146.
Magians, 7, 8, 10, 11, 165.
Magianism, 11, 165.
Maḥmūd, 88, 89, 90, 103, 105, 108.
Malachi, 17.
Mālik, 33, 34, 44.
Manael, 18.
Mani, 11, 12.
Marcus, 78, 95, 98.
Mary, 77, 80, 142.
Matthew, 55, 148-151, 161.
Media, 95, 97, 137.
Melchites, 157.
Micah, 118.
Midian, 94, 110, 119.
Miriam, 17.
Moses, 2, 16, 17, 28, 29, 30, 52, 55, 74, 75, 76, 77-87, 119, 137, 149, 158-159, 161, 162, 164.
Mshabbḥa, 130-131.
Mu'āwiah, 13, 43, 70.
Muḥammad, 1, 26, 39, 42, 75, 76, 79, 86, 88, 90, 92, 98, 102, 103, 105, 108, 110, 115, 119, 130-132, 134.
Mumajjad, 130-132.
Musabbaḥ, 130-132.
Musailamah, 11.
Muslim (Abu), 45.
Muslim (adj.), 19, 25, 38, 44, 47, 48, 55, 73, 110, 143.
Muslim (subs.), 3, 31, 33, 36, 41, 47, 49, 57, 58, 62, 63, 66, 71, 72, 75, 76, 95, 106, 117, 125, 145, 152, 153, 154, 155, 156, 168, 169.
Mutawakkil, 4, 19, 152, 168, 169.

N.

Nabatia, 97.
Nahum, 17.
Najāshi, 39.
Nebaioth, 110.
Nebuchadnezzar, 133.
Nestorians, 157.
Noah, 22.

P.

Pagans, 58, 163.
Paraclet, 140-141.
Paran (mount), 80, 86, 87, 119, 144.
Paul, 18, 55, 130, 144-145, 153, 160, 164.
Persia, 91, 97, 126.
Persian (language), 121, cf. 84.
Persian, 47, 50, 54, 84, 98, 126, 127, 137, 162.
Pharaoh, 81, 101, 155, 164.
Philip, 18.
Philistia, 154.
Phirūz, 46, 47.
Pilate, 150.
Pison, 90.
Protected cults (*dhimmis*), mainly 58 and 154-155.

R.

Rabī' (b. Khaitham), 72.
Refugees, 147.
Romans, 150.

S.

Sabeans, 7.
Sa'd (b. 'Ubādah), 38, 39.
Samuel, 154, 161.
Sarah, 78, 79, 83, 106, 130.
Satan, 12, 55, 59, 60, 165, 166.
Saul (Paul), 130.
Saul, 18.
Sawād, 126.
Seba, 89.

Seir, 86, 144.
Sheba, 89, 110.
Silas, 18.
Simon, 18.
Simon (Cephas), 55, 75, 83, 130, 142, 143, 148.
Sinai, 86, 144.
Sind, 46, 114.
Sinim, 112.
Solomon, 55.
Syria, 73, 76, 82, 101, 121, 126, 144, 154, 162.
Syriac, 87, 103, 116, 121, 129, 130, 131, 141.
Syrian, 87, 95, 129, 154.
Sudan, 121.
Sufyān (Abu), 34.
Sūs, 58, 82.

T.

Tabābi'ah, 7, 126.
Tabari (the author), 1.
Ṭabaristán, 84.
Ṭarshish, 89, 93, 111.
Thamūd, 72.
Tibet, 58.
Tigris, 90, 100.
Timothy, 164
Tradition, 17, 42, 46, 162.
Trinity, 123, 159, etc.
Tubba', 126.
Turanians, 156.
Turkestan, 58, 82.
Turks, 106, 122, 157.

U.

Ukaidir, 39.
'Ukkāshah, 32.
'Umar, 33, 42, 45, 47, 62, 63, 65-68.
'Umar (b. Abd al-'Azīz), 70-72.
Umayyads, 46, 70, 126.
'Uthmān, 33, 42, 43, 45.

W.

Walīd (b. Mughīrah), 31.
Walīd (b. Yazīd), 70.
War (Holy, *Jihād*), 23, 49, 57, 143, 153-157, 167.

Y.

Ya'la (b. Umayyah), 35.
Yaman, 46, 47, 90, 101, 110.
Yazīd, 70.

Z.

Zakkār (Abu), 147, 148, 152.
Zechariah, 123.
Zephaniah, 121, 123.
Zindīḳism, 165.
Zindīḳs, 7, 10, 51.
Zion, 53, 116.
Zoroaster, 10, 12.
Zubair, 43.

ABERDEEN: THE UNIVERSITY PRESS

PUBLICATIONS
OF
THE JOHN RYLANDS LIBRARY

CATALOGUES, HAND-LISTS, DESCRIPTIVE NOTES AND TRANSLATIONS OF, OR RELATING TO, MANUSCRIPTS IN THE JOHN RYLANDS LIBRARY.

CATALOGUE OF THE DEMOTIC PAPYRI IN THE JOHN RYLANDS LIBRARY. With facsimiles and complete translations. By F. Ll. Griffith M.A. 1909. 3 vols. 4to. 5 guineas *net.*

Vol. 1: Atlas of facsimiles in collotype. Vol. 2: Lithographed hand copies of the earlier documents. Vol. 3: Key-list, translations, commentaries, and indexes.

*** This is something more than a catalogue, since it includes collotype facsimiles of the whole of the documents, with transliterations, translations, valuable introductions, very full notes, and a glossary of Demotic, representing, in the estimation of scholars, the most important contribution to the study of Demotic hitherto published.

CATALOGUE OF THE COPTIC MANUSCRIPTS IN THE JOHN RYLANDS LIBRARY. By W. E. Crum M.A. 1909. 4to, pp. xii, 273. 12 plates of facsimiles, in collotype. 1 guinea *net.*

*** The collection includes a series of private letters considerably older than any in Coptic hitherto known, in addition to many manuscripts of great theological and historical interest. Many of the texts are reproduced *in extenso.*

NEW COPTIC MANUSCRIPTS IN THE JOHN RYLANDS LIBRARY. By W. E. Crum. 1920. 8vo, pp. 7. 1s. *net.*

*** Descriptive notes of a few Coptic pieces on papyrus and vellum which have been acquired since the publication of the aforementioned catalogue in 1909.

CATALOGUE OF THE GREEK PAPYRI IN THE JOHN RYLANDS LIBRARY. By Arthur S. Hunt, M.A., Litt.D., J. de M. Johnson, M.A., and Victor Martin, D. ès L. Vol. 1: Literary texts (Nos. 1-61). 1911. 4to, pp. xii, 204. 10 plates of facsimiles in collotype. Vol. 2: Documents of the Ptolemaic and Roman periods (Nos. 62-456). 1916. 4to, pp. xx, 488. 23 plates in collotype. Each volume 1 guinea *net.*

*** The texts are reproduced *in extenso*, and comprise many interesting Biblical, liturgical, classical papyri, and non-literary documents of an official or legal character ranging from the third century B.C. to the sixth century A.D.

CATALOGUE OF THE LATIN MANUSCRIPTS IN THE JOHN RYLANDS LIBRARY. Nos. 1-183. By Montague Rhodes James, Litt.D., etc. 2 vols. 4to. 187 plates of facsimiles. 4 guineas *net.*

Vol. 1: Descriptive catalogue, with indexes of contents, place names, proper names, saints, illustrations, etc. Pp. xvi, 328.

Vol. 2: Facsimiles in collotype.

*** The collection here described includes examples, of first-class quality, of the art and calligraphy of most of the great writing schools of Europe.

HAND-LIST OF ADDITIONS TO THE COLLECTION OF LATIN MANUSCRIPS IN THE JOHN RYLANDS LIBRARY, 1908-1920 (Nos. 184-332). By R. Fawtier, D. ès L. 1921. 8vo, pp. 21. 1s. *net.*

*** The MSS. dealt with in this temporary hand-list represent the additions, to the number of 149, to the Latin section of the Western MSS., which were acquired for the library between the years 1908 and 1920. They include several very important service books, cartularies, wardrobe books, and other interesting historical and theological items.

HAND-LIST OF THE MAINWARING AND JODRELL MANUSCRIPTS, at present in the custody of the John Rylands Library. By R. Fawtier, D. ès L. 8vo, pp. 48. 2s. *net.*

*** The collections dealt with have been deposited in the library, on loan, for safe custody, and include a number of interesting early charters (many of which date back to the time of Edward I.), diaries, household books, literary papers, and other deeds and evidences relating to the Cheshire estates and families of Mainwaring, who have been seated in Cheshire ever since the Conquest, and of Jodrell, who have been seated there certainly since 1357.

HAND-LIST OF THE SYRIAC MANUSCRIPTS IN THE JOHN RYLANDS LIBRARY. By A. Mingana, D.D. 1922. 8vo, 2s. *net.* [*Nearly ready.*

*** The collection is not a large one, but it includes a number of interesting works of permanent value, notably: a copy of Gannath Bussāmé, the unpublished repertory of East Syrian exegesis; chapters from the first work ever written on monasticism by Gregory of Cyprus; the Capita of Nestorius; an unique lexicographical treatise; two treatises dealing with India, one by an eye-witness describing the landing of the Portuguese, and their successive misfortunes and final success; a transcript of the oldest extant text of the liturgical prayers of the Nestorians, written in China, etc. The hand-list contains many descriptive notes.

SUMERIAN TABLETS FROM UMMA IN THE JOHN RYLANDS LIBRARY. . . . Transcribed, transliterated, and translated by C. L. Bedale, M.A. . . . With a Foreword by Canon C. H. W. Johns, M.A., Litt.D .1915. 4to, pp. xvi, 16, with ten facsimiles. 5s. *net.*

*** This thin quarto consists of a description of fifty-eight tablets, forming part of the collection recently acquired by the library.

BRIEF NOTES ON SOME OF THE RARER OR UNIQUE ARABIC AND PERSIAN-ARABIC MANUSCRIPTS IN THE JOHN RYLANDS LIBRARY. By A. Mingana, D.D. 1922. 8vo, pp. 9. 1s. *net.*

*** The object of these notes is to direct attention to works of importance in the particular field of research to which they belong, the very existence of which would otherwise remain unknown until the full catalogue, which is in preparation, is published; since the whole of the items dealt with are either unique or of such rare occurrence as to render them almost so.

AN IMPORTANT OLD TURKI MANUSCRIPT IN THE JOHN RYLANDS LIBRARY. By A. Mingana, D.D. 1915. 8vo, pp. 12, with two facsimiles. 1s. *net.*

*** The MS. referred to is a trilingual copy of the Kurân in fourteen volumes. The languages, which are interlinear, are Arabic, Persian, nnd Old Turki.

"FILIA MAGISTRI": un abrégé des sentences de Pierre Lombard. Notes sur un manuscrit latin conservé à la Bibliothèque John Rylands. By Raymond M. Martin, O.P. 1915. 8vo, pp. 12. 1s. *net.*

SOME EARLY JUDÆO-CHRISTIAN DOCUMENTS IN THE JOHN RYLANDS LIBRARY. 1. A new life of Clement of Rome; 2. The Book of Shem, Son of Noah; 3. Fragment from the Philosopher Andronicus and Asaph, the Historian of the Jews. Syriac Texts edited with translations by A. Mingana, D.D. 1917. 8vo, pp. 62. Boards, 2s. net.

THE BOOK OF RELIGION AND EMPIRE. A semi-official defence and exposition of Islām, written by order at the Court and with the assistance of the Caliph Mutawakkil (A.D. 847-861). By Ali Tabari. Translated with a critical apparatus from an apparently unique MS. in the John Rylands Library by A. Mingana, D.D. 8vo, pp. xxiv, 174. Cloth, 10s. 6d. *net.*

*** Hitherto, as far as we have been able to ascertain, no such apology of Islam, of so early a date, and of such outstanding importance, by a learned Muhammadan doctor, has been known to exist. The work is of first-rate importance to the Muslim, and not of less importance to every oriental scholar, whilst to those interested in theological questions it cannot fail to be of interest. It follows generally the "Apology of the Christian Faith" of Al Kindi, which the author probably intended to refute. It contains about 130 long Biblical quotations to prove the divine mission of the prophet, which follow the Syriac version of the Bible, said in the MS. to have been translated by "Marcus the Interpreter," who may probably be identified with "Mark the Evangelist," who is credited by a Syriac authority with having made a translation of the Old Testament into Aramaic or Syriac.

CATALOGUES OF PRINTED BOOKS IN THE JOHN RYLANDS LIBRARY.

CATALOGUE OF THE PRINTED BOOKS AND MANUSCRIPTS IN THE JOHN RYLANDS LIBRARY. 1899. 3 vols. 4to, cloth. 31s. 6d. net.

*** A brief-title author catalogue of the printed books, including the Althorp collection, and the few manuscripts with which the library shelves were equipped at the time of its inauguration.

CATALOGUE OF BOOKS IN THE JOHN RYLANDS LIBRARY PRINTED IN ENGLAND, SCOTLAND, AND IRELAND, and of Books in English printed abroad to the end of the Year 1640. 1895. 4to, pp. iii, 147. Cloth, 10s. 6d. *net.*

*** A brief-title author catalogue, with an index of printers, under which is a chronological list of books printed by them.

THE ENGLISH BIBLE IN THE JOHN RYLANDS LIBRARY, 1525 to 1640. By Richard Lovett. 1899. Fol, pp. xvi, 275, with twenty-six facsimiles in collotype, and thirty-nine engravings. Bound in full morocco. 5 guineas.

*** Of this sumptuous volume only 100 copies were printed for private circulation by Mrs. Rylands. Very few copies remain.

A CLASSIFIED CATALOGUE OF THE WORKS ON ARCHITECTURE AND THE ALLIED ARTS IN THE PRINCIPAL LIBRARIES OF MANCHESTER AND SALFORD, with alphabetical author list and subject index. Edited for the Architectural Committee of Manchester by Henry Guppy, M.A., and Guthrie Vine, M.A. 1909. 8vo, pp. xxv, 310. 3s. 6d. *net*, or interleaved 4s. 6d. *net.*

*** This catalogue is the first of its kind to be issued, with the exception of a few union lists of periodicals and incunabula.

THE JOHN RYLANDS FACSIMILES.

A series of reproductions of some of the more interesting and important of the rarer books in the possession of the library. The volumes consist of minutely accurate facsimiles of the works selected, preceded by bibliographical introductions.

PROPOSITIO JOHANNIS RUSSELL, printed by William Caxton, *circa* A.D. 1476. . . . With an introduction by Henry Guppy, M.A. 1909. 8vo, pp. 36, 8. 3s. 6d. *net.*

*** An oration, pronounced by John Russell, Chancellor of England, on the investiture of Charles, Dukeof Burgundy, with the Order of the Garter, in February, 1469, at Ghent. For many years the copy now in the John Rylands Library was considered to be unique. Until 1807 it lay buried and unnoticed in the heart of a volume of manuscripts, with which it had evidently been bound up by mistake. Since then, another copy has been discovered in the library at Holkam Hall, the seat of the Earl of Leicester.

A BOOKE IN ENGLYSH METRE, of the Great Marchaunt man called "Dives Pragmaticus". . . . 1563. . . . With an introduction by Percy E. Newbery, M.A.; and remarks on the vocabulary and dialect with a glossary by Henry C. Wyld, M.A. 1910. 4to, pp. xxxviii, 16. 5s. *net.*

*** The tract here reproduced is believed to be the sole surviving copy of a quaint little primer which had the laudable object of instructing the young in the names of trades, professions, ranks, and common objects of daily life in their own tongue.

A LITIL BOKE the whiche traytied and reherced many gode thinges necessaries for the . . . Pestilence . . . made by the . . . Bisshop of Arusiens. . . . [London], [1485 ?]. . . . With an introduction by Guthrie Vine, M.A. 1910. 4to, pp. xxxvi, 18. 5s. *net.*

*** Of this little tract, consisting of nine leaves, written by Benedict Kanuti, or Knutsson, Bishop of Västerås, three separate editions are known, but only one copy of each, and an odd leaf are known to have survived. There is no indication in any edition of the place of printing, date or name of printer, but they are all printed in one of the five types employed by William de Machlinia, who printed first in partnership with John Lettou and afterwards alone in the City of London, at the time when William Caxton was at the most active period of his career at Westminster.

WOODCUTS OF THE FIFTEENTH CENTURY IN THE JOHN RYLANDS LIBRARY. Reproduced in facsimile. With an introduction and descriptive notes by Campbell Dodgson, M.A. Folio. Ten plates, of which two are in colour, and 16 pp. of text, in a portfolio. 7s. 6d. *net.*

*** Two of these woodcuts are of exceptional interest and importance, and have been known and celebrated for a century and a half, but have not hitherto been reproduced in a satisfactory manner by any of the modern photo-mechanical processes. The two woodcuts referred to represent "St. Christopher" and "The Annunciation," the former of which has acquired a great celebrity by reason of the date (1423) which it bears, and which, until recently, gave to it the unchallenged position of the first dated woodcut.

THE ODES AND PSALMS OF SOLOMON. Facsimile in collotype of the original Syriac manuscript in the John Rylands Library, accompanied by a typographical reprint or transliteration of the text, a revised translation in English Versicles, and an exhaustive introduction dealing with the variations of the fragmentary manuscripts in the British Museum, the accessory patristic testimonies, and a summary of the most important criticisms that have appeared since its first publication in 1909. By J. Rendel Harris, M.A., D.Litt., etc., Hon. Fellow of Clare College, Cambridge, and Alphonse Mingana, D.D. 2 vols. 4to.

Vol. 1 : The text, with facsimile reproductions. 10s. 6d. *net.*

Vol. 2 : Translation and introduction. 1 guinea *net.*

MISCELLANEOUS PUBLICATIONS.

THE JOHN RYLANDS LIBRARY: A Brief Record of Twenty-one Years' Work (MCM-January MCMXXI). By Henry Guppy, M.A. 8vo, pp. xiv, 58, with forty-three views and facsimiles. One Shilling *net*.

*** This was written to commemorate the library's coming of age.

A BRIEF HISTORICAL DESCRIPTION OF THE JOHN RYLANDS LIBRARY, and its Contents. By Henry Guppy, M.A. 1914. 8vo, pp. xvi, 73, with thirty-seven views and facsimiles. One shilling *net*.

AN ANALYTICAL CATALOGUE OF THE CONTENTS OF THE TWO EDITIONS OF "AN ENGLISH GARNER," compiled by Edward Arber (1877-97), and rearranged under the editorship of Thomas Seccombe (1903-04). Edited by Henry Guppy, M.A. 1909. 8vo, pp. viii, 221. One Shilling *net*.

THE ASCENT OF OLYMPUS. By J. Rendel Harris, M.A., D.Litt., etc. Demy 8vo, pp. 140. 20 Illustrations. 5s. *net*.

*** A reprint, with corrections, expansions, justifications, and additional illustrations, of the four articles on Greek Mythology, Aphrodite, Apollo, Artemis, and Dionysos, which have appeared in the "Bulletin" from time to time.

THE EVOLUTION OF THE DRAGON. By G. Elliot Smith, M.A., M.D., F.R.S., etc. 1919. Demy 8vo, pp. xx, 234, with 26 plates and many illustrations in the text. Cloth. 10s. 6d. *net*.

*** An elaboration of three lectures delivered in the John Rylands Library on "Incense and Libations," "Dragons and Rain Gods," and "The Birth of Aphrodite".

AILRED OF RIEVAULX AND HIS BIOGRAPHER, WALTER DANIEL. By F. M. Powicke, M.A., Litt.D. 1922. 8vo, pp. vi, 112, with facsimile. 3s. 6d. *net*.

*** Compiled, translated, and edited from a twelfth century MS. recently acquired by the John Rylands Library, nnd another MS. in Jesus College, Cambridge.

THE BULLETIN OF THE JOHN RYLANDS LIBRARY. Edited by the Librarian.

It appears twice each year, in the months of January and July. The numbers usually run to about 150 pages, and are often illustrated with facsimiles and other pictorial matter. 2s. *net* each

It is now in its seventh volume, but all the preceding volumes (except the first) are still procurable as follows: Vols. 2, 1914-15 (4 parts), 4s. *net*; 3, 1916-17 (4 parts), 4s. *net*; 4, 1917-18 (4 parts), 4s. *net*, 5, 1918-20 (5 parts), 6s. *net*; 6, 1921-22 (4 parts), 8s. *net*.

*** This publication was commenced in 1903, with the object of providing a medium of communication between the library, its readers and others who might be interested in its work, and at the same time of revealing to students and lovers of literature the opportunities for research which such a library holds out.

It was continued by annual issues until 1908, when by reason of the exigencies of other work it was found necessary to suspend publication.

In October, 1914, publication was resumed in response to repeated inquiries, which seemed to reveal the need for some such link between the library and those in various parts of the world who were interested in its operations.

Such was the enthusiastic welcome accorded to the "Bulletin" in its revived form, that we were encouraged to make an attempt to develop its literary character, and in this we have been successful through the assistance of a number of scholars, who have very generously furnished us with a regular succession of original articles, the outstanding importance of which may be gathered by a glance at the accompanying list of reprints. In this way a place has been assured to it amongst the periodicals of a genuine literary standing.

REPRINTS OF ARTICLES WHICH APPEARED ORIGINALLY IN THE "BULLETIN OF THE JOHN RYLANDS LIBRARY."

With scarcely an exception these monographs embody the results of new and original investigations by scholars of the highest eminence, who have thereby imparted a fresh stimulus to study in their respective fields of research.

Demy 8vo. One shilling *net* each, unless otherwise stated.

CLASSICAL.

CONWAY (R. S.), Litt.D., F.B.A. The Youth of Vergil. 1915. Pp. 28.

—— The Philosophy of Vergil. 1922. Pp. 18.

—— The Venetian Point of View in Roman History. 1917-18. Pp. 2[illegible].

—— The Portrait of a Roman Gentleman from Livy. 1922. Pp. 16.

GRENFELL (B. P.), D.Litt., F.B.A. The Present Position of Papyrology. Pp. 21.

HARRIS (J. RENDEL), Litt.D., D.Theol., etc. The Origin of the Cult of Aphrodite. 1916. Pp. 30. With 9 illustrations.

—— The Origin of the Cult of Appolo. 1916. Pp. 40. With frontispiece and illustrations.

—— The Origin of the Cult of Artemis. 1916. Pp. 39. With illustrations.

—— The Origin of the Cult of Dionysos. 1915. Pp. 17. With illustrations.

—— The Origin and Meaning of Apple Cults. 1919. Pp. 52. With illustrations. 2s.

SOUTER (ALEXANDER), M.A., D.Litt. List of Abbreviations and Contractions, etc., in the John Rylands Library Latin Manuscript, No. 15. 1919. Pp. 7.

HISTORICAL.

BRUTON (F. A.), M.A., Litt.D The Story of Peterloo. Written for the centenary, 16th August, 1919. 8vo, pp. 45. With plates. 2s.

HARRIS (J. RENDEL), Litt.D., D.Theol., etc. Three Letters of John Eliot and a Bill of Lading of the "Mayflower". 1919. 8vo, pp. 11. With frontispiece.

PERRY (W. J.), B.A. War and Civilisation. 1917-18. 8vo, pp. 27. With 9 Sketch Maps.

POWICKE (FREDERICK J.), M.A., Ph.D. Eleven Letters of John, Second Earl of Lauderdale (and First Duke), 1616-82, to the Rev. Richard Baxter (1615-91). 1922. 8vo, pp. 33.

THUMB (A.). The Modern Greek and his Ancestry. 1914, 8vo, pp. 27.

TOUT (T. F.), M.A., Litt.D., F.B.A. The Captivity and Death of Edward of Carnarvon, 1920, 8vo, pp. 49. 2s.

—— The English Civil Service in the Fourteenth Century. 1916. 8vo, pp. 32.

—— Mediæval and Modern Warfare. 1919. 8vo, pp. 28.

—— A Mediæval Burglary. 1915. 8vo, pp. 24. With illustrations.

—— Mediæval Forgers and Forgeries. 1920. 8vo, pp. 31.

—— Mediæval Town Planning. 1917. 8vo, pp. 35. With 11 illustrations. 2s.

SMITH (G. ELLIOT), M.A., M.D., F.R.S., etc. The Influence of Ancient Egyptian Civilisation in the East and in America. 1916. Pp. 32. With 7 illustrations.

LITERARY.

HERFORD (C. H.), M.A., Litt.D., etc. Gabriele d'Annunzio. 1920. Pp. 27.

—— National and International Ideals in the English Poets. 1916. Pp. 24.

—— Norse Myth in English Poetry. 1919. Pp. 31.

—— The Poetry of Lucretius. 1918. Pp. 26.

—— Recent Tendencies in European Poetry. 1921. Pp. 27.

—— Some Approaches to Religion through Poetry during the past Two Generations. 1922. Pp. 33.

GUPPY (HENRY), M.A., D.Phil. A Brief Sketch of the Life and Times of Shakespeare. With a Chronological Table of the principal Events. 1916. Pp. 30 With frontispiece.

—— Dante Alighieri, 1321-1921. An appreciation, in commemoration of the Six-hundredth Anniversary of the Poet's Death. Pp. 13. With 3 facsimiles.

POEL (WILLIAM). Prominent Points in the Life and Writings of Shakespeare. Arranged in four tables. 1919. Pp. 12.

—— Some Notes on Shakespeare's Stage and Plays. 1916. Pp. 16. With 3 illustrations.

THEOLOGICAL.

BUCKLE (D. P.), M.A. The Forty Martyrs of Sebaste. A Study of Hagiographic Development. 1921. Pp. 9. With 4 facsimiles.

HARRIS (J. RENDEL), Litt.D., D.Theol., etc. Metrical Fragments in iii. Maccabees. 1920. Pp. 13.

—— Celsus and Aristides. 1921. Pp. 13.

—— Marcion's Book of Contradictions. 1921. Pp. 21.

—— Stoic Origins of the Fourth Gospel. 1922. Pp. 13.

HOSKIER (H. C.). Manuscripts of the Apocalypse: Recent Investigations. Part I. 1922. Pp. 20. With 5 facsimiles.

MINGANA (A.), D.D. Synopsis of Christian Doctrine in the Fourth Century according to Theodore of Mopsuestia. 1920. Pp. 21.

PEAKE (A. S.), M.A., D.D., etc. The Quintessence of Paulinism. 1917-18. Pp. 31.

—— The Roots of Hebrew Prophecy and Jewish Apocalyptic. 1923. Pp. 28.

—— The Movement of Old Testament Scholarship in the Nineteenth Century. Synopsis of a Lecture in the John Rylands Library on Nov. 11, 1903. With some leading Dates in Pentateuch Criticism. 1903. Pp. 8.

—— Bibliographical Notes for the Study of the Old Testament. 1913. Pp. 7.

—— Bibliographical Notes for Students of the New Testament. 1914. Pp. 10.

POWICKE (FREDERICK J.), M.A., Ph.D. A Puritan Idyll; or, Richard Baxter's Love Story. 1917. Pp. 35.

—— The Story and Significance of the Rev. Richard Baxter's "Saints' everlasting rest". 1920. Pp. 35. With frontispiece.

MISCELLANEOUS.

JAMES HOPE MOULTON, 1863-1917. 1. A Biographical Sketch, with some Account of his Literary Legacies. By W. Fiddian Moulton, M.A. 2. A Record of Professor J. H. Moulton's Work, with some explanation of its significance. By A. S. Peake, M.A., D.D. 3. Letter from Dr. Rendel Harris to the Rev. W. Fiddian Moulton. 1917. Pp. 18. With portrait.

ESSEN (L. VAN DER). La Bibliothèque de l'Université de Louvain. . . . Steps towards the reconstruction of the Library of the University of Louvain. [By H. Guppy.] 1915. Pp. 16.

HARRIS (J. RENDEL), Litt.D., D.Theol., etc. The Woodpecker in Human Form. 1920. Pp. 17.

RIVERS (W. H. R.). Dreams and Primitive Culture. 1917-18. Pp. 28.

—— Mind and Medicine. Second edition. 1920. Pp. 23.

EXHIBITION CATALOGUES.

CATALOGUE OF THE MANUSCRIPTS, BOOKS, AND BOOK-BINDINGS EXHIBITED AT THE OPENING OF THE JOHN RYLANDS LIBRARY, October 6th, 1899. 1899. 8vo, pp. 41. [*Out of print.*

THE JOHN RYLANDS LIBRARY: a brief description of the building and its contents, with a descriptive list of the works exhibited in the main library. By Henry Guppy. 1902. 8vo, pp. 47.

CATALOGUE OF AN EXHIBITION OF BIBLES IN THE JOHN RYLANDS LIBRARY, illustrating the history of the English versions from Wiclif to the present time. Including the personal copies of Queen Elizabeth, General Gordon, and Elizabeth Fry. 1904. 8vo, pp. 32. 1s. *net.*

A BRIEF HISTORICAL DESCRIPTION OF THE JOHN RYLANDS LIBRARY AND ITS CONTENTS, with catalogue of the selection of early printed Greek and Latin classics exhibited on the occasion of the visit of the Classical Association in October MCMVI. 1906. 8vo, pp. 89. With plates. 1s. *net.*

CATALOGUE OF AN EXHIBITION OF BIBLES IN THE JOHN RYLANDS LIBRARY, illustrating the history of the English versions from Wiclif to the present time, including the personal copies of Queen Elizabeth, Elizabeth Fry, and others. 1907. 8vo, pp. vii, 55. With plates. 1s. *net.*

CATALOGUE OF THE SELECTION OF BOOKS AND BROADSIDES ILLUSTRATING THE EARLY HISTORY OF PRINTING, exhibited in the John Rylands Library on the occasion of the visit of the Federation of Master Printers and Allied Trades in June, MCMVII. 1907. 8vo, pp. v, 34. [*Out of print.*

CATALOGUE OF AN EXHIBITION OF ILLUMINATED MANUSCRIPTS, PRINCIPALLY BIBLICAL AND LITURGICAL, exhibited in the John Rylands Library on the occasion of the meeting of the Church Congress in October, MCMVIII. 1908. 8vo, pp. vii, 62. With plates. 1s. *net.*

CATALOGUE OF AN EXHIBITION IN THE JOHN RYLANDS LIBRARY OF THE ORIGINAL EDITIONS OF THE PRINCIPAL WORKS OF JOHN MILTON, arranged in celebration of the tercentenary of his birth. 1908. 8vo, pp. 24. 1s. *net.*

CATALOGUE OF AN EXHIBITION OF THE WORKS OF DANTE ALIGHIERI, shown in the John Rylands Library from March to October, MCMIX. 1909. 8vo, pp. xii, 55. 1s. *net.*

CATALOGUE OF AN EXHIBITION OF ORIGINAL EDITIONS OF THE PRINCIPAL ENGLISH CLASSICS, shown in the John Rylands Library from March to October, MCMX. 1910. 8vo, pp. xv, 64. 1s. *net.*

CATALOGUE OF AN EXHIBITION OF MANUSCRIPTS AND PRINTED COPIES OF THE SCRIPTURES, illustrating the history of the transmission of the Bible, shown in the John Rylands Library from March to December, MCMXI. Tercentenary of the "Authorised version" of the English Bible: A.D. 1611-1911. 1911. 8vo, pp. xiv, 128. With plates. [*Out of print.*

CATALOGUE OF AN EXHIBITION OF MEDIÆVAL MANUSCRIPTS AND JEWELLED BOOK COVERS, shown in the John Rylands Library from January XII to December, MCMXII, including Lists of Palæographical Works and of Historical Periodicals in the John Rylands Library. 1912. 8vo, pp. xiii, 134. With plates. 1s. *net.*

A BRIEF HISTORICAL DESCRIPTION OF THE JOHN RYLANDS LIBRARY AND ITS CONTENTS, with Catalogue of a Selection of Manuscripts and Printed Books exhibited on the occasion of the visit of the Congregational Union of England and Wales in October, MCMXII. With illustrations. Edited by Henry Guppy. 1912. 8vo, pp. x, 143. [*Out of print.*

CATALOGUE OF AN EXHIBITION IN THE JOHN RYLANDS LIBRARY OF THE WORKS OF SHAKESPEARE, his sources, and the writings of his principal contemporaries. With an introductory sketch by Henry Guppy, and sixteen facsimiles. Tercentenary of the death of Shakespeare, April 23rd, 1916. 1916. Second edition. 8vo, pp. xvi, 169. 1s. *net.*

Lightning Source UK Ltd.
Milton Keynes UK
174625UK00004B/60/P

9 781149 298879